MEXICO
at the
Crossroads

MEXICO
at the
Crossroads

Politics, the Church,
and the Poor

Michael Tangeman

ORBIS BOOKS
Maryknoll, New York 10545

The Catholic Foreign Mission Society of America (Maryknoll) recruits and trains people for overseas missionary service. Through Orbis Books, Maryknoll aims to foster the international dialogue that is essential to mission. The books published, however, reflect the opinions of their authors and are not meant to represent the official position of the society.

Copyright © 1995 by Michael Tangeman
Published in the United States by Orbis Books, Maryknoll, NY 10545
Manufactured in the United States of America

Queries regarding rights and permissions should be addressed to:
Orbis Books, P.O. Box 308, Maryknoll, NY 10545–0308

Cataloging-in-Publication Data is available from
the Library of Congress, Washington, DC

ORBIS/ISBN 1-57075-018-1

To the memory of Penny Lernoux

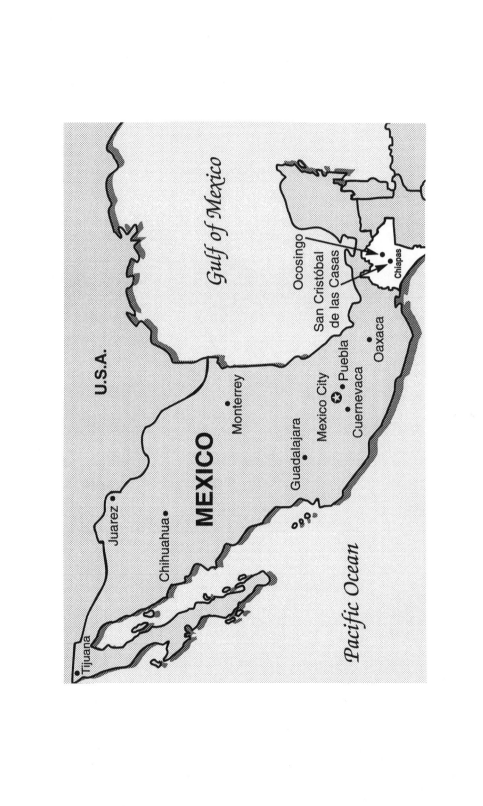

Contents

Preface

W HEN MY EDITOR at Orbis Books first suggested the title for this book, I was uneasy at the thought of fixing Mexico to a crossroads. After all, at the pace things were proceeding in 1994, it seemed possible that by the time the book appeared in the bookstores Mexico might have sped right through the crossroads — with or without any clear change of direction. Then, I remembered that back in June 1985 Bishop Arturo Lona Reyes of Tehuantepec told me that the Mexican church then was at a "crossroads," that the church hierarchy faced the choice of "continuing the reforms of Vatican II — which threaten the status of some priests and bishops — or of trying to restore the old order." At about the same time, Lona and five other Mexican bishops of the church's Southern Pacific region were pointing to another "crossroads," for Mexican society. In a pastoral letter entitled *Evangelization and Worldly Goods*, they urged Mexico's economically powerful to share more than their "leftovers" with the poor, telling them that "unshared wealth implies a denial of the kingdom of God, of the poor, and of salvation."

Perhaps more than any other event in recent memory, Mexico's January 1994 Zapatista rebellion by poor and indigenous subsistence farmers points to the fact that each and every day Mexican society and the Catholic Church continue to pull up to the same crossroads, to face the same dilemma: how to deal with the contradiction of a society where nearly half the population lives below the official poverty line, while a powerful elite grows wealthier by the day — so much so that from 1991 to 1994 alone, the number of Mexican billionaires grew from two to twenty-four! This concentration of wealth in the hands of a powerful elite is tied to the sweeping economic and political restructuring that has taken place in Mexico since 1988. As a result of that restructuring, Mexican society recently has gone through a remarkable amount of tension, polarization, and violence — beginning with the May 1993 murder of Cardinal Juan Jesús Posadas Ocampo, through the Zapatista uprising, tense national elections, the 1994 assassinations of two top leaders of the ruling Institutional Revolutionary Party, a major peso devaluation and renewed economic crisis..

This book is an attempt to examine how the Catholic Church — laity, religious, priests, and bishops — has dealt with the challenge of situating itself in relation to the poor and the powerful each time Mexico has pulled up to the "crossroads" throughout its history. Today, as in the past, Mexican Catholicism — the religion to which some 85 percent of all Mexicans still profess fidelity — is being presented with an opportunity to define itself: Does the Mexican church live up to the inclusive concept of "people of God" in the spirit of the church's watershed Vatican Council II? Or has it become bound through its peculiar history of semi-legal existence to an institutional identity of the past — where a hierarchy that commands from above is most concerned with the status of the institutional church in society? And does it live its expressed "preferential option" for the unemployed and underemployed poor and working class, who make up a majority of the faithful — or is it aligned with those who exercise economic and political power at the expense of the majority?

This book attempts to dispel some of the myths and misconceptions that hinder an understanding of the Mexican Catholic Church: the notion that the Cristero rebellion of the 1920s was a hierarchy-directed uprising by reactionary and ignorant peasants; the idea that the spread of Evangelical Protestant churches is either part of a U.S.-financed conspiracy or represents a grave threat to Catholic hegemony in Mexico; and, most of all, that the Mexican church and its hierarchy can easily be defined along "conservative" and "progressive" political lines. While generalizations are sometimes helpful, bishops who are "conservative" on some issues as often as not end up being "progressive" on others: for example, Archbishop Carlos Quintero Arce, long accused of being a "conservative" promoter of the opposition National Action Party in his northern state of Sonora, has shown himself to be remarkably "progressive" on issues related to Central America and the rights of Central American refugees; on the other hand, notably "progressive" Bishop Samuel Ruiz toed the Vatican line and closed ranks with fellow prelates in 1990 when women's groups and the local government tried to depenalize abortion in his southern state of Chiapas.

If cultural blinders prevent one's being a prophet in one's own land, then it may be true that being a foreigner can provide the necessary distance to look at a culture or society from a fresh perspective. There are, undoubtedly, many Mexicans who have spent much more time than I contemplating church issues in Mexico and who are much closer to the Mexican church. However, I trust that by having lived and worked in Mexico for a decade, writing about Mexican Catholicism for much of that time, I am able to provide the reader with an insight into the realm of religion and politics in Mexico not easily found elsewhere. I expect that some of the information and points of view contained in this book will be of discomfort to more than a few, especially to many Catholics. To them, I can only say that I do believe that the truth —

as close as we can come to it in this world of ours — does "set you free," however painful it may be at times. As such, I believe the Catholic Church is ultimately strengthened by honest examination of its shortcomings and weakened when its faults are closeted away due to a false sense of institutional loyalty.

In the time I have reported on politics and religion in Mexico and Central America, I have received help from countless people — Catholics, mainstream Protestants and Evangelicals, journalists, academics, and social activists — without whose help my understanding of the subject would today be considerably more limited. To all of them, as to those Mexican bishops who have taken my phone calls at all hours of the day and night, and to the underpaid and overworked staff of Documentación e Información Católica (DIC), always helpful in providing information, my sincere gratitude. My editors on the foreign news desk at Catholic News Service in Washington, D.C., Bill Pritchard and Barb Fraze, also deserve recognition for their many years of editing my copy and the confidence they have always displayed in my knowledge and understanding of the church "story" in Mexico.

In the writing of this book, there are individuals who have been particularly helpful and to whom I owe special thanks. First and foremost, I must especially thank my wife, Margaret Hooks, always an inspiration to me as both journalist and author, without whose encouragement and help I might never have undertaken this book, much less completed it. To all those who gave of their time in interviews or provided me with key information, my sincere gratitude, in particular: José Alvarez Icaza; Pedro Arellano; Miguel Concha, O.P.; Eduardo García; Rogelio Gómez Hermosillo; Pablo Iribarren, O.P.; Gonzalo Ituarte, O.P.; Manuel Jara; Aurora López, O.S.F.; Eugenio Maurer, S.J.; Patricia Moysen, S.V.Z.; Pablo Romo, O.P.; Adolfo Suárez Rivera; Samuel Ruiz García; Jorge Trejo, O.P.; Kathy Vargas; Olga Vargas, O.P.; Alberto Velázquez, S.J.; and Jesús Vergara, S.J. Among my colleagues and friends, many thanks to Andrew Paxman, who encouraged me at a crucial juncture to undertake this project; to Lucy Conger, for having allowed me to see part of the manuscript for her forthcoming book on human rights in Mexico; and to José Antonio Román at La Jornada, for his generosity over the years in sharing information and his own insight into the Mexican Catholic Church. Special thanks also to my Latin American Studies professors and to Guillermo Westphal, for his having introduced me to México profundo.

In the ecumenical spirit of Vatican II, I must also thank my extended family — which has included Catholics, Jews, fundamentalist Christians, Lutherans, Presbyterians, and agnostic humanists — for having through their very diversity been a constant reminder of the need to remain open to the points of view of many faiths in writing this book. Thanks also to my editors at Orbis Books, Robert Ellsberg and Catherine Costello, and to Maryknoll, for making the project a reality. And, finally, my deepest gratitude to my parents, George and Irene Tangeman, and to the teachers of my youth, to whom I owe more than I can possibly express here for having instilled in me the sense of religious humanism that inspired this book.

Abbreviations

ACM	Mexican Catholic Action
CCRI	Indigenous Clandestine Revolutionary Committee
CEB	Basic Christian Community
CECRUN	Critical University Center
CEE	Ecumenical Studies Center
CELAM	Latin American Bishops Council
CEM	Mexican Bishops Conference
CENAMI	National Center for Aid to Indigenous Missions
CENCOS	National Center for Social Communications
CEPI	Bishops Commission on Indigenous Peoples
CEPS	Bishops Commission on Social Work
CFE	Federal Electoral Commission
CIOAC	Independent Central Organization of Agricultural Laborers and Campesinos
CLAR	Latin American Confederation of Religious
CND	National Democratic Convention
CNDH	National Human Rights Commission
CNS	Catholic News Service
COCEI	Coalition of Workers, Campesinos, and Students of the Isthmus
CON	Confederation of National Organizations
CONAI	National Mediating Commission
COSYDDHAC	Commission in Solidarity and Defense of Human Rights
CROM	Regional Mexican Workers' Confederation
CTM	Confederation of Mexican Workers
DEA	U.S. Drug Enforcement Administration
EMP	Presidential Guard
EZLN	Zapatista National Liberation Army
FAC	Foundation for Assistance to the Community (previously Catholic Assistance Fund)
FAR	Armed Rebel Forces (Guatemala)

FDN	National Democratic Front
FDS	Federal Security Directorate
IFE	Federal Electoral Institute
IMF	International Monetary Fund
IPN	National Polytechnic Institute
JOC	Young Catholic Workers
MFC	Christian Family Movement
NAFTA	North American Free Trade Agreement
OCEZ	Emiliano Zapata Campesino Organization
PAN	National Action Party
PCM	Mexican Communist Party
PCN	National Catholic Party
PEMEX	Petróleos Mexicanos
PNR	National Revolutionary Party
PRD	Party of the Democratic Revolution
PRI	Institutional Revolutionary Party
PRM	Mexican Revolutionary Party
PROCAMPO	National Program of Direct Rural Aid
PRONASOL	National Solidarity Program
PRT	Revolutionary Workers Party
PSE	Economic Solidarity Pact
PSM	Mexican Socialist Party
PSUM	Mexican Unified Socialist Party
SEDENA	National Defense Secretariat
SEDESOL	Secretariat of Social Development
SERESURE	Regional Seminary of the Southeast
SIL	Summer Language Institute
SSM	Mexican Social Secretariat
UMAE	Bishops Mutual Aid Union
UNAM	National Autonomous University of Mexico
URNG	Guatemalan National Revolutionary Unity
UU	Union of Unions

1

Rebellion in the Promised Land

S HORTLY BEFORE MIDNIGHT on New Year's Eve, Father Eduardo García trudged back down the road into the small mountain town of San Andrés Larraínzar. "Go back, there'll be no fighting here," the masked leader of the armed group had told him. "We're headed for San Cristóbal." A diocesan priest assigned since 1991 to this town of mostly Tzotzil Mayan sub-sistence farmers in the southern Mexican state of Chiapas, Father "Lalo" had come to Larraínzar to spend the night and rise for Mass early on New Year's Day. He had never seen such agitation in San Andrés as upon his arrival, when the local people had come to tell him that strange men had entered the town and cut the sole telephone line and CB radio antennas, which linked the town to the outside world.

Later he had watched from a prudent distance at the fork in the road above the town as a rapidly increasing number of armed Tzotzil men and women clad in green and brown uniforms, their faces covered with ski masks or red bandanas, assembled alongside a dozen or more vehicles comman-deered from the municipal president's office. Now, as the order was given to board the rag-tag caravan that would carry them the fifteen miles to the outskirts of San Cristóbal de las Casas, the regional capital of the Chiapas highlands, Father Lalo headed back into the center of Larraínzar, wonder-ing to himself what was going on, a question he would continue to ask throughout the early hours of that fateful first day of 1994.

Seventy-five miles away, across the pine-covered mountains in the town of Ocosingo, a group of priests and nuns at the Dominican mission parish of San Jacinto de Polonia were bringing in 1994 with a traditional midnight dinner. New Year's Eve had been cold and calm for the customary celebra-tion of Mass at ten o'clock. As the dinner ended around 2:00 A.M., Sister Olga Vargas prepared to leave along with the other Dominican nuns and Franciscan Sister Aurora López. But as the large metal gate to the street swung open, they beheld a scene that snatched their breath away: from the shadows of the street corner a group of masked gunmen peered out from the darkness, their weapons trained upon the central plaza and their objective beyond, the Ocosingo town hall and the dozens of policemen barracked inside.

Slamming the gate shut, the nuns ran quickly to the rectory, where together with the Dominican priests they switched on the parish's CB radio. "What in the world is going on?" thought Father Jorge Trejo. Recalling veiled threats from local Tzeltal and Chol Mayan Indians that "war" would break out over the reigning social injustice in the region, Father Jorgito wondered aloud: "What if it really is true?" For the next two hours, the priests and nuns listened as taxi drivers and judicial police reported sightings of armed groups all over town. Then, by 4:00 A.M., there was virtual silence on the airwaves. Whoever they were, whatever their aim, the armed individuals had vanished — or so it seemed.

Ironically, it was Pope John Paul II's annual message of peace that Bishop Samuel Ruiz García had stressed in his homily during the nine o'clock New Year's Eve Mass in San Cristóbal's cathedral. After Mass, exhausted from the stress of the preceding days, Bishop Ruiz had lay down to rest when he was disturbed by the ring of the telephone shortly after midnight. The call was unwelcome, but the caller's tone was urgent: a group of armed men were at the northern outskirts of San Cristóbal, on the road coming from Chamula and Larraínzar. Ruiz suggested that they were probably just holiday revelers firing their pistols into the air — the traditional one round for each month of the year. No, insisted the caller, it seemed to be something altogether different. Another call within minutes told the bishop that an armed contingent was marching in formation toward the cathedral and main square. When a group of about ten heavily armed men knocked at the door of the diocesan curia sometime later, Ruiz refused to answer, concerned that their aim might be to take him and the diocesan offices hostage. As dawn approached, although unable to directly observe the events taking place in the town hall and main square from the curia, Bishop Ruiz became only too aware that he was right in the middle of what was clearly a perilous situation.

Meanwhile, as day broke in Larraínzar, Father Lalo and some friends were anxiously tuning their radio set to the regional station XEOCH in Ocosingo. As the signal became clear, they heard the same broadcast being listened to by the nuns in Ocosingo, the same heard by Bishop Ruiz and diocesan staffers in the San Cristóbal curia: interspersed with lively *ranchera* music, individuals named "Ovidio," "Uno," and "Virginia" announced that the highlands and jungle of Mexico's southern state of Chiapas were at war: a revolutionary group calling itself the Zapatista National Liberation Army (EZLN), having risen in arms against the Mexican military, demanded the ouster of Mexican President Carlos Salinas de Gortari and rejected the implementation of the North American Free Trade Agreement (NAFTA) between Mexico, the United States, and Canada, due to take effect that very day. Throughout the morning, the captured radio station in Ocosingo broadcast the rebels' "Lacandón Jungle Declaration," detailing their demands for social justice in Chiapas, democratic freedoms nationwide, and the repeal of NAFTA, which the rebels decried as a potential "death certificate"[1] for Mexico's indigenous groups and *campesino* subsistence farmers.

The taped message verified what had been seen by the Dominican priests as they had opened the doors of the San Jacinto parish church at daylight onto an Ocosingo town square fully occupied by Zapatistas. It also coincided with the shock felt by Sister Patricia Moysen and the other hospital Sisters of Charity of St. Vincent de Paul an hour away in the town of Altamirano, when the early morning silence was broken by the sound of gunfire coming from the police checkpoint outside town. Zapatista raids on the Altamirano town hall, the local ranchers' association, and the headquarters of the governing Institutional Revolutionary Party (PRI) followed, with the shootout subsiding an hour later. Summoned from the hospital, Sister Patricia fetched the wounded, including two of three critically injured policemen.

Zapatista combatants brought a dozen of their own casualties; then their local field commander arrived, a young *mestiza,* a non-Indian Mexican woman of mixed blood, accompanied by two indigenous women combatants. Introduced by her *nom de guerre,* "Comandante Alejandra," she proceeded calmly and methodically to explain to everyone at the hospital the Zapatista manifesto. Sister Patricia never sensed it as such, but Alejandra's presence turned the hospital into a de facto Zapatista command post, a circumstance later used by detractors to try to link the nuns to the rebellion.

It was precisely such attempts at linking the church to the rebels that Bishop Ruiz hoped to avoid in San Cristóbal, where he remained inside the curia throughout New Year's Day and January 2, as indigenous Zapatista troops led by a charismatic mestizo calling himself "Subcomandante Marcos" occupied the center of town. Monitoring events via telephone, radio, and television, Bishop Ruiz soon became aware that the rebels had also attacked or occupied the towns of Las Margaritas, Altamirano, Chanal, and Ocosingo and the military base at Rancho Nuevo. The telephone in the curia did not stop ringing for the next five days as Mexico and the world took note of the surprise indigenous rebellion. Sometime during the long hours of January 1, 1994, Bishop Ruiz realized that his role as pastor of the diocese of San Cristóbal de las Casas had been irrevocably altered by what would soon come to be known as Mexico's "New Year's Rebellion."

Roots of Unrest

In a way, the rebellion was both a culmination and setback to a pastoral program that preached social justice with peace, one that Bishop Ruiz had introduced to the diocese nearly thirty-four years earlier, when in January 1960 he was ordained bishop of Chiapas by Pope John XXIII. A native of Guanajuato state in the heartland of traditional Mexican Catholicism, in 1960 the promising thirty-five-year-old Ruiz, with just ten years in the priesthood, seemed suited to join a traditionalist Mexican Bishops Conference (CEM), one that later the same year reacted to Fidel Castro's incipient persecution of the Cuban church by roundly rejecting communism and the socialist view of the world. But personal background and hierarchical dispositions aside, it was the timing of Ruiz's ordination — one year to the day from John XXIII's call for a Second Vatican Council to modernize the Catholic Church — that influenced how he approached his pastoral tasks.

If the diocese's twenty-six thousand square miles of jungle, mountains, and coastal plains complicated the task of spreading the Gospel, the problem was further compounded by an appalling socio-economic morass. Statewide, the birth rate was just beginning a spiral out of control with a jump over the previous decade of 3.35 percent. Of every thousand infants born, some sixty-six died within twelve months, primarily from disease and malnutrition. The overall annual mortality rate of 12.3 deaths per 1,000 inhabitants topped Mexico's national average, and 56 percent of the state's population was unable to read or write, ranking Chiapas as one of the worst three states nationwide in terms of illiteracy.[2]

Some two hundred thousand Mayan Indians, the original inhabitants of Chiapas, lived a precarious existence in the impoverished and over-crowded highlands around San Cristóbal. These mostly Tzeltal and Tzotzil communities of subsistence farmers, along with the closely related Chols, Tojolobals, Zoques, and Lacandóns, were the poorest in an extremely poor state. With an average highland population density five times the state average and as many as 209 inhabitants crowded into a single square mile in some cases, the Indians worked small plots in mountain villages that barely sustained their families. Many rented fields in the coastal foothills to augment their harvests or traveled for seasonal work to lowland coffee and cotton plantations at less than the daily minimum wage of a dollar a day. Still more left to pioneer the "national lands" being opened to settlers by the government in the Lacandón jungle.[3] Locking the indigenous groups into poverty was deep-seated racial discrimination by a political and economic elite of *ladinos,* non-Indians of both Mexican and foreign descent. Bishop Ruiz still remembers the revulsion he felt in the 1960s at seeing Indians forced off the sidewalks of San Cristóbal just to let ladinos pass.[4]

The young bishop soon found that the roots of those problems sunk deep in the history of Chiapas, Mexico, and the Catholic Church itself. After all, the church had used the same cross of evangelization in conjunction with the sword of the Spanish conquistadors to exploit and discriminate against Indians for centuries. Following the Spanish conquest of the Aztecs in 1521, the European invaders moved south and in 1524 subjugated the highland Mayans with the defeat of the Tzotzils at Chamula. As a result, descendants of Maya-speakers that had begun their emigration to highland Chiapas with the decline of classical Mayan civilization in the tenth century c.e. faced an onslaught against their very identity, as the Spaniards attempted to dominate them culturally, politically, and spiritually.

On the site of present-day San Cristóbal, the Spaniards established their regional capital, Ciudad Real, then dependent upon the Captaincy General of neighboring Guatemala. The city was consecrated in 1539 as the see of the diocese of Chiapas, and in 1544 a Spanish-born Dominican priest, Bartolomé de las Casas, already well-known for his criticism of the brutal treatment of Indians in the colony of New Spain, was ordained as the first bishop of Chiapas. Arriving in 1545 with the first Dominicans to evangelize the region, Fray Bartolomé was a notable, if brief, exception to the general rule of church complicity in the conquest. His vehement protests against the abuses under the *encomienda* system of tributary labor prompted his recall to the mother country. There he continued to battle those who tried to justify the inhumane treatment of the Indians with the argument that they possessed neither a soul nor the power of reason. Forced to resign his post as bishop, Las Casas never returned to Chiapas and died in Spain in 1566.

Sadly, despite Fray Bartolomé's legacy, within a few short years of his departure the Dominican order had lapsed into the very vices he had criticized. By the end of the sixteenth century, with an essentially slave work force of Indians, the Dominicans had constructed ninety monasteries and churches throughout southern Mexico and Central America. Moving beyond the immediate Tzotzil and Tzeltal zone around San Cristóbal, impoverished and disease-stricken Indians erected churches for the Dominican order among the Chols at Tila, Tumbalá, and Palenque and built their monasteries among the Zoques at Tecpatán and Chapultenango and at the Tojolobal-Tzeltal settlement of Balun Canan (present-day Comitán).

Employing a variety of mechanisms, some authorized by the Crown, others clearly illicit, the Dominicans joined non-clerical landowners in appropriating vast expanses of indigenous land. By the end of the colonial period, the order had amassed extensive *haciendas* and cattle ranches in the subtropical valleys and canyons around Palenque, Ocosingo, and Tila and the fertile valleys of Comitán, La Trinitaria, and Las Margaritas.[5] In the half century of turmoil that followed Mexico's independence from Spain in 1821 (and Mexico's annexation of Chiapas from Guatemala shortly thereafter), such church properties were lost under a series of reform laws. However, the zeal of Mexico's nineteenth-century liberals for individual ownership precluded legal recognition of communal landholding, and the ancestral lands of the Mayans of Chiapas were not returned to them.

On the contrary, even more lands were taken under a law granting as much as a third of supposedly vacant rural lots, known as *terrenos baldíos*, to anyone who took the trouble to survey them. Unscrupulous ladino land sharks took advantage of the indigenous practice of leaving a portion of their fields fallow to claim that the fields were abandoned. They then surveyed, applied for, and received title to the property, forcing the Mayan farmers further out of fertile valleys and onto steep slopes, where erosion and rocky soil meant lower crop yields and greater poverty. Under dictator Porfirio Díaz, who ruled the country virtually uninterrupted from 1877 to 1911, vast expanses of the supposed *terrenos baldíos* that had accrued to the government were sold off to domestic and foreign investors. In the thirty-five years preceding the Mexican Revolution of 1910–17, nearly 4.5 million acres of land which once belonged to the Mayans of Chiapas wound up in the hands of Mexican- and foreign-owned lumber, coffee, rubber, and oil companies.[6]

For the Indians of Chiapas, revolutionary peasant leader Emiliano Zapata's rallying cry of "land and liberty" rang hollow after the Revolution of 1910–17, as local elites swapped a pledge of loyalty to northern revolutionary chieftains for virtual exemption from land reform. Exploitation of Chiapas's natural resources by private investors thus continued unabated through the 1940s, with lumber companies advancing steadily into the canyons leading to the Lacandón jungle. The result was the beginning of a major demographic shift, with highland Indians whose fields were exhausted being recruited by the companies to cut the precious tropical hardwoods. Chols, Tzeltals, and Zoques moved down the densely vegetated canyons from Palenque, Ocosingo, and Altamirano, denuding the hillsides for their employers, as did the Tojolobals in the canyons of Comitán, La Trinitaria, and Las Margaritas. Later, the Tzotzils followed, leaving behind overpopulated villages around Chamula and San Cristóbal.

While the largest timber companies began to scale back operations or pull out of the region by the mid-1950s, the highland Indians they had contracted stayed on, slashing and burning the jungle to make way for their small plots of maize. With increased population pressure in the highlands posing a potential political problem, the federal government chose a populist solution and encouraged migration, granting settlers title to communal ejido farmland in the fast-receding jungle. The exodus thus increased rapidly, and joining in the odyssey were not only highland Mayan villagers but many Indians still living as virtual serfs on coffee *fincas* originally owned by Spaniards — some of which even belonged once to the Dominicans.

Toward an Indigenous Christianity

But in fact the economic and physical presence of the Dominicans and other religious orders had long since nearly vanished completely from Chiapas. By the mid-eighteenth century, the Spanish Crown had curtailed the mendicant orders' dominance of the early church, replacing them with diocesan clergy at the parish level. Post-independence expropriation of the orders' agrarian holdings combined with a shortage of diocesan clergy left vast expanses abandoned by the church. In 1963, when Bishop Samuel Ruiz invited U.S. Dominicans to re-establish the order's abandoned Ocosingo mission, they found that for nearly a century lone diocesan priests had the impossible task of taking the sacraments on burro-back to hundreds of villages spread over thousands of square miles.

Even so, the natural religiosity of the Tzeltals had not been damped by the lack of an institutional church, as the first Jesuits to set up a mission in the abandoned parish of Chilón-Bachajón found in 1958. Inside the Bachajón church, the local Tzeltals had safeguarded their Catholic saints, revering them in their own fashion — along with a carved stone stela, salvaged from the Mayan ruins at Tila, believed sacred by the Indians. The worship of the stela provides a glimpse of the highland Mayans' myriad forms of resistance to European cultural domination. But perhaps the clearest testimony to that spirit of resistance is the litany of armed indigenous insurrections that occurred from 1525 through the nineteenth century. Religious symbols were elements in many of the rebellions, such as the Tzotzil "War of the Castes" (1867–70), in which many of the insurgents were united by a cult centered on stones deemed to hold divine powers, and a Tzeltal rebellion in 1712–13, caused by abuses by the local bishop and with church refusal to sanction reported apparitions of the Virgin Mary in the Tzeltal village of Cancuc.

Although in 1960 there existed an indigenous majority within the diocese — with a fervent religiosity expressed through an incipient "Mayan Christianity"[7] — scant regard was still being paid to indigenous culture. Bishop Ruiz's arrival and his growing enthusiasm for the "opening" signified by Vatican II led to the expansion of the missionary spirit begun at Chilón-Bachajón and the training of indigenous catechists already begun under Ruiz's predecessor. The then-novel ideas of accommodating the institutional church to the social and historical realities of the faithful and of increasing the participation of the laity meant but one thing for Bishop Ruiz in Chiapas: a greater incorporation of the indigenous population in the life of the church.

Soon Ruiz invited other religious orders to help out in the diocese: beginning in 1961 Franciscans were active among the Chols near Palenque, two years before the Dominicans of the Holy Name Province of California took up their mission at Ocosingo, which they ran in tandem with U.S. Maryknoll nuns and lay missionaries. Jesuits, Dominicans, and diocesan clergy and religious began to virtually compel villagers to select candidates for instruction in catechesis; schools for catechists run by Marist brothers were established in 1961, and within seven years some seven hundred indigenous catechists had been trained.[8] Meanwhile, the diocese began to set up rural cooperatives, elementary health-care projects, and credit unions in indigenous areas with the help of a Mexican church agency dedicated to social service. The laity was brought into the process through *cursillos de cristiandad*, basic workshops on Christian living, then being organized nationwide through the Movement for a Better World.

The advances were significant, but the diocesan pastoral team sensed something was lacking in their "Western, top-down approach"[9] to evangelization. Some indigenous communities complained outright that diocesan-trained catechists, although indigenous, did too much preaching *at them*. Searching for a different model, the diocese found its watershed in the historic 1968 Medellín conference of the Latin American Bishops Council (CELAM). Medellín's emphasis on prophetic denunciation of systemic injustice and the insertion of the church in the realities of the poor provided a "liberating proclamation"[10] for the diocese, prompting two fundamental changes in approach: first, the church began to focus on identifying structural mechanisms that kept indigenous people poor; second, it decided to try to "humbly learn how the Spirit of God lives and acts in the values and the redeeming historical events of [indigenous] culture."[11]

In the process, church workers began to focus more on indigenous people themselves, with diocesan pastoral workers taking anthropology courses and studying indigenous culture and religiosity. The Jesuit and Dominican missions at Chilón-Bachajón and Ocosingo found that in the absence of the Western notion of "teacher" in the Tzeltal language, there nevertheless existed a more holistic concept of "one who helps another to learn."[12] In 1971, they changed their catechetical methods accordingly, dropping traditional indoctrination in favor of collective reflection on the meaning of scripture. With catechists stimulating community participation instead of simply "teaching" catechesis, the method came to be called *tijwanej* (meaning "to agitate," or "to move" in Tzeltal).[13] It spread to other diocesan pastoral zones, but among the Tzeltals the methodology evolved into a particularly appropriate catechesis based on the book of Exodus, entitled "Estamos buscando la libertad" (We are seeking freedom).[14] Through paragraph-by-paragraph reflection, Tzeltal communities encouraged by their catechists began to recognize their own oppression in the slavery of the Israelites, their own forced migration to the Lacandón jungle in the flight of God's chosen people toward the promised land.

In 1974, Samuel Ruiz was commissioned by Chiapas state governor Manuel Velasco Suárez to organize an indigenous congress on the five-hundredth birthday of Fray Bartolomé de las Casas. Because of its unpopularity, the government was unable to effectively convene such an event itself, but it apparently hoped for a folkloric "indigenist" affair. With the "*concientización*" process spurred by the new catechetical methods already underway, however, Ruiz and his pastoral team were determined the congress should be an opportunity for indigenous delegates to meet, reflect upon, and discuss their common reality. Organizers and indigenous coordinators set to work among the communities, and after months of preparation nearly two thousand indigenous delegates met in San Cristóbal in October 1974. Using participatory methods akin to those of *tijwanej* — and speaking to each other in indigenous languages via adolescent translators, who had learned all four languages in the multiethnic communities of the canyons of Las Margaritas and Comitán — delegates shed their traditional ethnocentrism and together identified and discussed four common problem areas: land tenure, health care, education, and the commercialization of agricultural products. Twenty years later, continued governmental neglect of the same areas would play a large part in the January 1994 Zapatista rebellion.

The year following the congress, a new twist occurred in the church's evangelization efforts when Tzeltal catechists pushed for a new ministry of indigenous deacons. First broached in the Chilón-Bachajón mission in 1972, the idea was for communities to choose a respected member already providing extraordinary community service as a candidate for the permanent diaconate, with power both to administer the sacraments and preside over traditional indigenous rituals. Finding legitimacy for the ministry in early church writings and the Vatican II documents *Lumen Gentium* and *Ad Gentes*, the diocese conditioned ordination upon a three-year trial period, during which candidates would be known as "pre-deacons." In 1975–76, Ruiz confirmed the communities' choices with ordination of dozens of pre-deacons. Called *tuhuneles* (meaning, simply, "servers" in Tzeltal), the new deacons represented a step toward spiritual empowerment of the highland

Mayans, a bold move toward an autochthonous church in an area in which European religious institutions had dominated since the conquest.

Enthusiasm for the new catechesis had grown concurrently with the indigenous congress, as communities reflected on a central theme: the discovery of God's plan for their salvation within the context of their political, economic, and historical realities of oppression and exodus. Accompanying that theme was the question of how to experience faith, hope, love, and charity in the face of such oppression.[15] Once their eyes were opened by the experience of the indigenous congress, the communities' common response to the question of how to experience Christian charity was startlingly similar: charity, they believed, could not be defined — it had to be lived. And how could it be lived? The breakdown of inter-ethnic barriers during the organization of the congress had shown them the way: true charity, they decided, is lived through solidarity; and true solidarity can be had only through organization.[16]

Organization and Repression

The immediate motivation for organizing themselves was that the "promised land" had come under threat. Thousands of migrants who had been encouraged by authorities to settle the canyons and jungle were now presented with an official about-face. In 1972, the federal government decreed nearly 1.5 million acres of jungle to be the property of just sixty-six Lacandón families. It then began to forcibly resettle thirteen Tzeltal and eight Chol communities on sites lacking services and plagued by unsanitary conditions. Ahead of the indigenous settlers the gate to the "promised land" was closed; behind them, non-indigenous cattle ranchers were encroaching on the lands that the ejido farmers had cleared.[17] In response, eighteen ejidos in an area immersed in the new catechesis founded *Quiptic ta (ach) lecubtesel* (our strength is unity for progress).[18] Legally recognized in 1976 along with two smaller ejido unions, Quiptic's aim was to protect land rights, and it successfully blocked relocation of twenty-six other Tzeltal and six Tojolobal communities. When a 1978 government decree restricted settlement in the 818,000-acre Montes Azules biosphere reserve and its 6.5 million-acre buffer zone, Quiptic grew rapidly, and by 1980 it represented some 120 communities.

The radicalism that eventually led to the 1994 Zapatista rebellion dates from this period. By 1978, a group of mestizo grassroots organizers from the northern city of Torreón arrived bearing a decidedly Maoist discourse and eventually attempted to co-opt the Quiptic movement. Invited by members of the diocesan pastoral team (apparently with the implicit blessing of Bishop

Ruiz himself),[19] the "Torreones" preached the democracy of the popular assembly, where everyone was equal and "leaders" were to be shunned. At first, the fervor of the itinerant assemblies of the "Torreones" caught on in the Tzeltal, Chol, and Tojolobal canyons. But the apparent anarchy of the Maoist approach clashed with indigenous traditions of community, and, by most accounts, the communities themselves expelled the "Torreones" in all but a few cases.[20]

Still, the northerners' efforts had a radicalizing effect. Faced with the threatened relocation of member communities, in 1980 Quiptic joined two other ejido alliances and campesino subsistence farmer groups to form the 180-community strong Unión de Uniones (UU). The UU's inception heralded a period of mass mobilization and marches on the state capital, Tuxtla Gutiérrez, with demands for land rights and better marketing conditions for small coffee producers. Into this rural ferment arrived another group of outsiders who filled the gap left by the "Torreones."

Confidential church sources say these people arrived unobtrusively and integrated themselves "just like missionaries," living in communities for years at a time, appearing to respect and even share indigenous spirituality, doing painstaking social work, planting and harvesting, sharing the Indians' pain and suffering. Mexicans by birth, mestizos in race and culture, inspired by revolutionary fervor in Central America, this relative handful of activists were believed by diocesan pastoral workers to have belonged to a larger Mexican organization and to have had links with neighboring Central American guerrilla organizations — indeed, they were probably involved in the ongoing arms smuggling throughout the 1980s via the canyons and jungles of Chiapas and across Mexico's southern border to the Armed Rebel Forces (FAR), one of four guerrilla groups operating in neighboring Guatemala. Ruiz and the diocesan team knew of the existence of this new group in Chiapas, but say they were never certain of their purpose: Were they disillusioned Mexican leftists given over to social work? Maoist *aventureros* with a strategy destined to failure? Or perhaps government agents, trying to foment unrest to co-opt or repress the emergent indigenous movement? No one seemed to know for sure.

Besides, there were other pressing issues at the time: the expulsions of Evangelical Christian converts from indigenous villages was virtually out of control, with nearly six thousand of the *expulsados* living in squatter settlements in and around San Cristóbal as of 1988. Defending them against the Catholic majorities in the villages, Ruiz realized that religion was being used to cover political and economic conflicts fomented by village powerbrokers, known as *caciques*. The diocese also played a key role in relief efforts to aid the approximately fifty thousand Guatemalan Mayan refugees living there since the early 1980s. Crowded into squalid camps, they were the victims of massive human rights abuses by the Guatemalan military in its counterinsurgency war against the umbrella Guatemalan National Revolutionary Unity guerrilla movement (URNG).

During the term of Governor Absalón Castellanos Domínguez (1982–88), an army general whose family reportedly acquired extensive landholdings in Chiapas, demonstrations and land takeovers were met with growing repression. From 1984 to 1987, uniformed and plainclothes state police joined by army troops frequently and brutally evicted members of the Independent Central Organization of Agricultural Laborers and Campesinos (CIOAC) and the Emiliano Zapata Campesino Organization (OCEZ) from occupied lands, and armed thugs and police were blamed for the murders of several land-rights activists, including one CIOAC lawyer.[21] In December 1987, one of the first clear reprisals for diocesan denunciation of the repression occurred when police raided a Maryknoll house in Comitán, accusing missionaries of the U.S. order of supporting CIOAC demonstrators.[22]

Despite hopes for change with the 1988 gubernatorial inauguration of Patrocinio González Blanco Garrido — a member of a large landholding family in the Chol region near Palenque and a cousin by marriage to President Salinas — repression sharply increased. Bishop Ruiz's response was to found the Fray Bartolomé de las Casas Human Rights Center in 1989. Legally independent of the diocese, yet located in the curia offices, the Fray Bartolomé Center's mere existence sharpened the Chiapas elite's loathing of Ruiz. In May 1990, their hatred overflowed as they used the occasion of Pope John Paul II's visit to Chiapas to publish an open letter accusing Ruiz of being a communist and of fomenting class hatred. Two months later, the diocese received a second clear warning when Belgian Father Marcel Rotsaert was deported on an immigration technicality and sixteen Guatemalan refugees arrested with him were jailed for fifty-seven days on unsubstantiated charges linked to a land takeover.[23] In July 1991, following a year of outspoken criticism of social injustices and denunciation of repression, diocesan priest Joel Padrón was arrested and held for forty-nine days on charges of promoting a CIOAC land takeover near his parish in Simojovel. With international attention focused on the jailed priest at a time of delicate church-state dialogue in Mexico City, Father Padrón declared from his prison cell that his only "crime" consisted of "encouraging Indians to stand up for their rights."[24]

While the church withstood the mounting pressures, the mestizo activists in the canyons and jungle were busy building a network of contacts among Tzeltal, Chol, and Tojolobal communities. Diocesan pastoral workers say that unlike the "Torreones," they showed a respect for indigenous community structures, always taking pains to seek an introduction to the community through an esteemed member — usually a catechist, a deacon, or the ejido representative. Ruiz himself has said that reports of arms being infiltrated into the jungle had alerted diocesan workers that something was afoot, but at the time "we didn't recognize either the magnitude or the proximity of events."[25] In time, the mestizos' offer of advice on organization and self-defense was subtly extended to include the offer of weapons and training so that the Indians could defend themselves against the mounting repression.

The acceptance was enthusiastic, with church sources confirming that by 1991 support for armed revolution had spread from the canyons to the highland Tzeltals of Tenejapa, the Tzotzils of Larraínzar, and most of the Tzotzil communities around San Cristóbal. While many communities were won over by the Zapatistas, the older generation of catechists and deacons began to doubt their intentions, their communities eschewing the shift from civil to violent resistance. But following a monumental 1992 reform to Article 27 of the Mexican constitution, many young and landless Indians quietly joined the armed movement. Designed by the Salinas administration to open up Mexico's agricultural sector to private investors in anticipation of NAFTA, among other things the Article 27 amendment virtually decreed an end to further redistribution of land and the granting of ejido titles. With the "promised land" once again under threat and some communities fearful that ejido land claims then under consideration would simply be rejected, the need for armed defense turned to a desire for armed revolt.

Bishop under Fire

As rights abuses grew during 1992, the Fray Bartolomé center expanded its contacts with a network of Mexican non-governmental rights groups and international human rights monitoring agencies. With outside pressure on the government over the Chiapas rights situation mounting, in June reports surfaced of a plot to assassinate Ruiz, allegedly hatched by the state's landowning elite. Governor González Garrido promised an official investigation, which predictably turned up no leads. Amnesty International specifically took up the cases of abuses against indigenous people in Chiapas, and although more than 60 percent of all Mexico's indigenous rights violations in 1992 occurred in the state, in January 1993 President Salinas chose González Garrido as federal Interior Secretary, placing him in charge of law enforcement and the national security apparatus. That same month, on the heels of a 1992 constitutional reform that ended a seventy-five-year ban against legal recognition of churches, Bishop Ruiz brought the Fray Bartolomé center fully under diocesan protection, registering it as a church agency with Dominican Father Pablo Romo as its director.

On March 20, three months after González Garrido's move to Mexico City, military officers, said to have stumbled onto a clandestine sawmill during an inexplicable "outing" near the Tzotzil village of San Isidro el Ocotal, were brutally murdered by unknown assailants. Nine days later, the army raided San Isidro looking for suspects and, without a warrant, arrested thirteen villagers, securing their "confessions" through beatings and torture. When the Fray Bartolomé center criticized the flagrant rights violations involved, local military commander General Miguel Angel Godínez Bravo lashed back, publicly charging the diocese with aiding and abetting murderers. Ruiz protested in a five-page letter asserting that even criminals have human rights that a Christian is bound to defend. But the damage had been done, and Ruiz's relationship with the authorities deteriorated beyond recovery.

Despite the denunciation over the case, the Fray Bartolomé center accepted the military's "sawmill" explanation given at the time. But the center's lawyer on the case and other informed sources in Chiapas later indicated that the officers had actually stumbled upon a Zapatista training camp, located within striking distance of the Rancho Nuevo military base. Nevertheless, the first official acknowledgement of the rebels' existence came later, after the army followed up a tip on a guerrilla camp near Ocosingo with an attack in late May that left one rebel and two soldiers dead. Amid the accompanying confusion, the Fray Bartolomé center remained cautiously silent until some six hundred state police returned without warrants on June 6 and raided four Tzeltal communities, beating villagers, confiscating weapons and personal belongings, and arresting twenty-five Tzeltal men.

Political considerations intervened, however, to spare the Zapatistas immediate confrontation with the full force of the Mexican military. On May 24, 1993, the country was sent into collective shock with the murder of Cardinal Juan Jesús Posadas Ocampo of Guadalajara in a shootout involving drug traffickers in that city's international airport. In neighboring Guatemala, President Jorge Serrano Elías's declaration of a state of emergency added to the tension in Mexico, contributing to a generalized climate of instability. In Washington, D.C., the U.S. Congress was on the verge of accepting Mexico as a partner in NAFTA, and free-trade opponents were looking for any excuse to disqualify the trade accord. Unwilling to admit the existence of any organized guerrilla movement in Mexico, President Salinas is believed to have personally decided to pull the Mexican army back from the jungle and have them deny that anything was amiss in Chiapas.

Clearly, at this late stage the diocesan defense of human rights had become a serious problem for those who exercised political, economic, and military power in Chiapas. In August, during Pope John Paul II's third visit to Mexico, Ruiz hand-delivered a pastoral letter to the pope, entitled "In This Hour of Grace." In it, he not only outlined the pastoral work in the diocese but thoroughly embarrassed the government with criticism of the Salinas administration's neo-liberal economic policies, drug-linked corruption among law enforcement agencies, and persistent racism, discrimination, and human rights abuses against Mexico's indigenous peoples. That letter may have been, as he later claimed, the last drop, "spilling out hatred accumulated in powerful corners" against him.[26] If so, then the late-September visit by Father Romo to Washington, D.C., where he testified on Chiapas rights abuses before the House of Representatives' Small Business Committee and met with NAFTA opponent Representative David Bonior and other U.S. congressional representatives, only added fuel to the fire.

If subsequent events are any indication, Ruiz's political enemies then launched their attack against him on the ecclesiastical front. On October 26, Archbishop Girolamo Prigione, the Vatican's long-term Mexico envoy whose collusion with a succession of Mexican Interior Secretariats is well-known, read Ruiz a letter from Cardinal Bernardin Gantin, prefect of the Vatican's Congregation for Bishops. The letter was written on September 23, just when Prigione happened to be visiting Rome, and in it Bishop Ruiz was criticized for the alleged use of "Marxist analysis" that resulted in a "reductionist view" of Christ and his teachings, and for having allegedly utilized a flawed doctrinal basis for diocesan pastoral work, which the letter termed "exclusivist." Oddly enough, the charges were said to be based on Ruiz's *ad limina* reports submitted every five years over the past thirty years, about which nothing had ever been said in the past. In an October 27 press conference at the elegant University Club in Mexico City, Prigione let reporters know in no uncertain terms that the allegations were serious enough to cause Ruiz's removal as bishop of San Cristóbal.

The result was a flurry of national and international messages of support for Ruiz that led the besieged Prigione to change the nunciature's telephone and fax numbers. In his pastoral letter delivered to the pope, Bishop Ruiz had already responded to the "exclusivist" charge, explaining that in its option for the poor, the diocese had not intentionally excluded the non-indigenous minority, but had been unable to find a methodology for reaching their hearts. "We are aware that many mestizos are opening their hearts; but we are also aware that many others are hardening theirs," he said.[27] As for the other charges, even non-partisans of liberation theology recognized "Marxist analysis" and "reductionism" as political red herrings rather than doctrinal questions.[28] They pointed out that even at the very height of the controversy over liberation theology in the church, with socialism and communism still alive and apparently well in the world, Vatican conservatives had been unable to bring one single Latin American liberation theologian to ecclesiastical trial on such charges.

Still, there was little alternative for Bishop Ruiz than to resign himself to a stormy stay in Rome during his upcoming *ad limina* visit in 1994. He cast about for some canonical legal defense and by Christmas had prepared his mandatory report to John Paul II. The surprise New Year's rebellion cut expected developments short, as fighting between the Zapatistas and Mexican army troops lasted for twelve bloody days in the Chiapas highlands and in the canyons leading to the Lacandón jungle. The fighting claimed the lives of some 165 people — Zapatistas, soldiers, and civilians — and the military's response to the uprising was marked by charges of serious human rights abuses against the civilian population and rebel prisoners.[29]

Following the Zapatistas' agreement to a cease-fire initially called by President Salinas, and after a presidential offer of amnesty, which was not taken up by the rebels, tense weeks ensued as the two sides discussed terms for negotiations. Held in late February, they turned out to be a kind of mute dialogue airing rebel demands and government responses. As the mediator in the negotiations, Bishop Ruiz saw his personal and pastoral destiny altered irrevocably, with the exigencies of a rapidly evolving post-rebellion political crisis propelling the Mexican Catholic Church into a leading role in the country's history for the first time in more than six decades.

2

From Conquest to Revolution

MORE THAN FOUR CENTURIES before Bishop Ruiz encouraged expression of indigenous Christianity in Chiapas, an important event occurred on a central Mexican hillside near the ancient Aztec capital of Tenochtitlán. Just a decade after Hernán Cortés and his four hundred conquistadors had vanquished the Aztec empire, Mesoamerican indigenous society was in shambles, its people humiliated by the Spaniards, their gods overcome by the God of the conquerors. On a December morning in 1531, just before dawn, a poor Nahuatl-speaking Indian, baptized "Juan Diego," was walking past the hill of Tepeyac, site of the pre-conquest shrine to the goddess Tonantzin, mother of all indigenous gods. Juan Diego's real name was Cuauhtlatoatzin, which is symbolic in Nahuatl for "he who relates the things of God," indicating that he may previously have been a figure of some importance — perhaps even an Aztec priest who had been suspended from his duties and reduced to the status of poor campesino by the conquest.[1]

According to the *Nican Mopohua*, a Nahuatl account written later by indigenous scholars at the Franciscan College of Santa Cruz of Tlatelolco, it was on the hill of Tepeyac that Juan Diego was overcome with awe by a divine apparition of the Virgin Mary. His lowly condition notwithstanding, the glorious figure of the Virgin affirmed Juan Diego's dignity by greeting him in the respectful Nahuatl form of "Juantzin, Juan Diegotzin." Identifying herself not only as "the ever-Virgin, Holy Mary," but specifically as the "mother of the God of Great Truth, Teotl," the Nahuatl name of the Indians' ancient god, the Virgin was adamant that a shrine be built in her honor — not in Tenochtitlán, the center of evangelization and domination by the conquering Spaniards, but on the hill of Tepeyac itself. From that site, she promised, she would love, aid, and defend the peoples of the New World in their hour of need.[2]

Engraved in Mexican consciousness as the miracle of the Virgin of Guadalupe is the story of how Juan Diego was subsequently able to convince Franciscan Bishop Juan de Zumárraga of the apparition's authenticity, aided by the supernatural appearance of the Virgin's image upon the garment he wore. The Virgin's name, "Guadalupe," was given her by the Spaniards after an Arabic place name near Cortés's home in the Spanish province of Extremadura, an obvious attempt at European co-optation of what was clearly an indigenous phenomenon. Mexico's Indians did not at first warm to the name change and referred to the Virgin as Tonantzin well into the next century. After all, this Virgin had chosen an Indian to spread the faith to other Indians, initiating a model of "bottom-up" evangelization that contrasted with the top-down imposition of Christianity by the Spaniards. Reasserting itself from time to time over the next four centuries, it was a model of evangelization born literally "of the people, by the people, and for the people" — those people who inhabited the New World when the Spaniards arrived and who would persist as the poorest and most defenseless of Mexico's inhabitants through the twentieth century.

When Cortés arrived in Mexico, there were an estimated 25 million indigenous people in Central Mexico alone. Chief among them were the Aztecs, a warlike people who in 1325 had ended a two-hundred-year trek from the north to settle on an island in Lake Texcoco, ringed by volcanic peaks in the valley of Mexico. The Aztecs managed through near-constant warfare to subjugate most of their neighbors, earning both obeisance and enmity while swelling their coffers through a lucrative tributary system.

Polytheistic and pluralistic religions were bound inextricably to all aspects of the lives of the peoples of Mesoamerica, from the Mayans in the south to the far northern nomadic tribes. Religious expression included worship of a pantheon of gods: those to whom official cults were established with elaborate temples and priestly castes; and the gods of the common people, patrons of the natural phenomena that were all-important in the ritual cultivation of the main food staples, maize and beans. Since the quality of life depended largely upon successful harvests, it was essential to appease the gods of nature, and most indigenous groups solicited their favor with blood offerings of human sacrifice. Victims were usually prisoners taken in battle, often conducted specifically for that purpose, making for an almost constant state of war.

The Cross and the Crown

Averse to neither war nor gore and driven by a greed for gold and a religious zeal born of an eight-hundred-year crusade in Spain against Islamic "infidels," the bearded Cortés and his band of armor-clad soldiers conquered the Aztecs and their allies in a series of shockingly bloody episodes. Accompanying the conquering sword — and the smoke of modern firearms — was the evangelizing cross of the Catholic Church. The Spanish cross and sword had been united since 1418 when, in return for a promise to drive Islam from the Iberian peninsula, Pope Martin V granted the Spanish Crown jurisdiction over all church affairs in Spanish territory. After Ferdinand and Isabel united Spain, this *patronato real* (royal patronage) grant was extended to all Spanish territories in the New World.

The first sandal-shod, coarse-clothed friars arrived in Mexico with Cortés, and others followed shortly thereafter. But in 1523 Cortés's zeal to convert the conquered led him to petition Spain's Hapsburg monarch and Holy Roman Emperor Charles V to send Dominican and Franciscan monks to "New Spain." In 1524, a dozen Franciscans arrived, followed in 1526 by the first Dominicans and a handful of Augustinians in 1533. A papal bull issued by Adrian VI gave the mendicant orders free reign wherever no bishop could be found, and they proceeded to divide up the colony for evangelization: the Franciscans from the capital generally westward, the Dominicans southward to Oaxaca, Chiapas, and Central America, and the Augustinians from Central Mexico toward the northeast.

The earliest evangelizers had a unique opportunity to recognize and accept uncanny parallels between indigenous and Christian beliefs. The Aztecs, for example, were familiar with the crucifix as a symbol of the four directions of the universe. They believed in virgin birth, their god of war Huitzilopochtli believed to have been born of the virgin goddess Teteoinan. They also believed in the immortality of the soul, had rituals vaguely resembling Christian baptism and communion, and even knew a kind of collective confession.[3]

Indeed, some of the first evangelizers were open to indigenous peoples and their ways. There were those whose concept of Christian charity led them to establish hospitals and schools; others believed indigenous customs and languages should be studied in order to Christianize the Indians in their own tongue, while leaving the rest of their culture intact. All three religious orders preached in Nahuatl, Mixtec, and Zapotec, and the Dominicans learned as many as ten Indian languages in their multilingual territory. Most notable was the Franciscan Bernardo de Sahagún, who showed fervent dedication to recording indigenous history, culture, customs, and language. The Franciscans' great mass-baptizer Fray Toribio de Benavente, "Motolinía," originally followed suit before acceding to the allures of power and becoming a bitter critic of Bartolomé de las Casas.

Fray Bartolomé and other Dominicans were most outspoken as defenders of the Indians' rights as human beings. Under the encomienda system, the Crown granted land and the labor of the indigenous people living on it to conquistadors and other Spaniards in return for their pledge to ensure both the welfare and Christian conversion of the royal subjects. In reality, however, the Indians simply became feudal vassals: Cortés's twenty-five thousand square miles of encomienda grants placed more than a hundred thousand Indians at his personal service.[4] Other conquistadors sold their Indians into certain death in the mines, while Nuño de Guzmán traded ten thousand encomienda Indians from Panuco as slaves in exchange for goods and livestock in the Antilles — one good horse reportedly fetching as many as a hundred Indian slaves.[5]

Before entering the priesthood in 1523, Las Casas was himself a small *encomendero* in Cuba. But after hearing the Dominican Fray Antonio de Montesinos preach against encomienda abuses in 1511, he experienced a conversion. Back in Spain, his defense of the Indians before an ailing Ferdinand and the young Charles V earned him the hatred of colonial encomenderos; this, however, was the impetus that later, after 1542, translated into slightly better treatment for Indians under the "New Laws of the Indies." It must be said that Las Casas's position was not entirely pure: for a time he favored black African slavery to better the lot of indigenous *encomendados*, and in 1546 he came out in favor of enslaving Indians who dared rise up against the Crown.[6] Nor were he and the Dominicans the only critics of the system: before becoming a Franciscan and first bishop of Mexico City, Zumárraga complained to Charles V of the abuse of slaves at Panuco; and the Augustinian Alonzo de Soria was pulled from the pulpit on his arrival in New Spain in 1533 for denouncing the slave trade.

The predominant view, however, considered the Indians inferior beings, the very existence of their souls and powers of reason debatable. Its impetus came from the Franciscans' medieval mentality, which saw indigenous and Christian religious similarities as Satan's work, designed to confound the task of evangelization. Even Sahagún was swayed by this view, denouncing the comparisons of the Virgin Mary with the goddess Tonantzin as a "satanic invention to justify idolatry."[7] Study of indigenous customs became a means to root out and destroy "superstition." Indigenous youth converted to Christianity were also coaxed to inform on their parents' adherence to the old religion; such was the case in Tlaxcala, where three young boys baptized Cristóbal, Antonio, and Juan were killed by their own people after having betrayed their families to church authorities. With royal permission to use the rubble of demolished temples to build monasteries and to erect churches atop the ruins, monks like Zumárraga and Fray Martín de la Coruña proudly tallied the number of idols and temples they had helped destroy.

By the 1570s, the influence of the first evangelizers was waning. The banished Las Casas had died in Spain; Sahagún's manuscripts on indigenous ways were confiscated and his writing on the subject prohibited. The church's Council of Trent (1545–63) forbade the ordination of Indians, mestizos, or blacks, while the same obsession with evil and doctrinal dissent that led to the torture and deaths of Jews and heretics in Europe brought the Inquisition to New Spain. Zumárraga had already burned Indian leader Carlos Moctezuma at the stake for idolatry before the arrival of the inquisitors, and the Holy Office promptly forbade the translation of scripture into indigenous languages. Mexico's first inquisitor, Pedro Moya de Contreras, later archbishop and interim viceroy, implemented Trent's emphasis on church hierarchy and order. The office of bishop was given renewed importance, and in 1574 the powers of the mendicant orders were curtailed through the Ordenanza de Patronazgo, granting the Crown absolute control over church appointments. It gradually "put the orders back into the monasteries," with secular clergy assuming control of most parishes in central Mexico by the early 1600s.[8]

The indigenous population not killed, worked to death, or sold into slavery was almost annihilated by European disease, against which they had no biological defense. Of the 25 million Indians of central Mexico in 1521, just over a million are believed to have survived by 1600. The Society of Jesus arrived in 1572 and — with the notable exception of Jesuit Bishop "Tata" Vasco de Quiroga, who organized the Purepecha Indians of Michoacán into utopian artisan communities — the Jesuits joined the other orders in profiting from the administration of Indians forced to relocate into settlements called *reducciones*. Supposed to facilitate more efficient evangelization, "civilization," and organization of the native work force, the reducciones served along with the *repartimiento* assignment of indigenous labor to enrich the orders via prosperous farming and ranching enterprises. From 1670 to 1751 in western Mexico, for instance, nearly a quarter of some nineteen thousand Indians working under the repartimiento system provided free labor to the church, with the Jesuits the main beneficiaries.[9]

Hapsburgs, Bourbons, and the New World

Throughout the seventeenth century, the Hispanic Hapsburg monarchs ruled their colonies with the same static, medieval concept of society as they ruled Spain. Large rural landholdings, monopolistic commercial practices, and bloated bureaucracies were the norm. Colonial wealth was measured solely in terms of exports to mother Spain, and the church collaborated in ensuring the success of the colonial enterprise. For its co-administration of outlying areas and provision of educational, hospital, and public registry services, the church obtained a 10 percent surcharge on all taxes collected, known as the *diezmo*. The tax swelled ecclesiastical coffers, and with the surplus capital the colonial church hierarchy bought up hacienda plantations, sugar mills, ranches, and urban rental properties. With its vast profits, the church began lending money and became "the banker and partner of agriculturalists, mine-owners, and businessmen, thus linking its interests with those of the minority that formed the tip of the social pyramid."[10]

Disturbed by the continuing genocide of potential New World vassals, the Hapsburgs attempted to protect the remaining Indians from their rapacious Spanish colonial subjects through a special arrangement called the República de las Indias. The laws of Castile continued to govern non-Indians, but the indigenous population was ruled under a commune system modeled on Spanish municipal government, with communities annually electing "republican officials" who collected tribute and assigned labor service for the Crown. Although the plan was neat in theory, corruption prevailed in practice, with viceregal officials often awarding elections to the highest indigenous bidder or to one who would deliver free labor to abusive Spanish *hacendados* or the clergy.

By the 1650s, the indigenous population is believed to have reached its lowest level and begun a slow comeback. Continued abuse by the Spaniards led to sporadic but short-lived revolts, from Chiapas in the south to Durango and Coahuila in the north. In Mexico City, Indians and mestizos revolted in the face of inhumane treatment by Spaniards on at least three occasions from 1624 to 1697. Either despite or because of the Indians' hardship, indigenous religiosity during the period flourished in new ways. Construction of shrines to Catholic saint-substitutes for indigenous deities proliferated with the clergy's encouragement, as did the founding of religious confraternities dedicated to patron saints. Elaborate fiestas developed, linked to the ancient rituals of the agricultural cycle or in honor of patron deity-saints, and the pre-Hispanic practice of pilgrimages to sacred shrines continued — a statue of Christ, the Virgin, or a saint now occupying the place of the ancient idol.

When the last Spanish Hapsburg, Charles II, died heirless in 1700, France's Louis XIV placed his nephew Phillip of Anjou on the Spanish throne, passing control of Spain and its colonies to the French Bourbon dynasty. Europe was entering the eighteenth-century Enlightenment, and the new Spanish monarchs hoped through their "Bourbon renaissance"[11] to modernize the administration of Spain's possessions. Citizen farmers were favored over large landholders, middle-class merchants were preferred over trade monopolies, and productive enterprise was considered more desirable than gross extraction of primary materials. Phillip V finally suppressed the encomiendas in 1720, making way for the private hacienda estates, with their absorption of indigenous villages and substitution of encomienda tribute by debt peonage as the principal means of exploiting Indians. After a lengthy economic depression in the colony, in the 1750s Charles III commissioned a series of studies to streamline the economy and royal bureaucracy. But while the Bourbons instituted progressive economic and administrative policies, they were still absolute monarchs — and their suspicion of corporate entities that threatened Crown authority tinged their policies with an anti-clerical cast.

They were particularly troubled by the Jesuits, who openly defended church supremacy against the new liberal ideas of the Enlightenment. The Jesuits' special ministry was to the generations of Spanish subjects born in the colonies, known as *criollos,* and the order was overly influential in colonial society. The Jesuits had also amassed a sizeable fortune, with Pope Innocent X receiving complaints as early as 1647 that the Jesuits owned the "best haciendas" in New Spain, some "very rich silver mines," and twice as many sugar mills as the rest of the church combined.[12] Furthermore, through cadres like Swiss-born Jesuit Francisco Eusebio Kino, who established innumerable missions on some forty expeditions to the far north, the order became a key factor in expansion of colonial religious and political authority.

But the Bourbons were also disturbed by the Jesuits' role in spreading the notion that the criollos had an identity all their own, distinct from Spaniards born on the Iberian peninsula. Criollos enjoyed greater status than either Indians or mixed-blood mestizos, but were clearly second-class subjects when compared to the *peninsulares.* In promoting a criollo sense of identity, the Jesuits used a powerful symbol — the Virgin of Guadalupe — and encouraged criollos to see the Virgin's unique choice of Mexico for her apparition as "irrefutable" proof of their equality or even superiority to peninsulares.[13] But in adopting her as their own symbol, the criollos also spawned what some have seen as an essentially "classist and racist"[14] cult of Guadalupe, rejecting the fact that her message was originally addressed to the oppressed Indians, abused by the criollo perhaps more than any other.

When Charles III reacted to increasing Jesuit wealth and influence by summarily expelling the order from all Spanish colonies in 1767, consequent political unrest climaxed in a revolt in the mining center of Guanajuato, mercilessly suppressed by Crown troops. Criollo pride was wounded but was soon assuaged with the economic prosperity spurred by new "progressive" economic and administrative policies enacted in 1775. The reforms were successful, but the Bourbons had other problems, not least of which was encroachment on their New World territories by other European powers. Military expeditions to the north, accompanied by missionaries like Franciscan Father Junípero Serra, who from 1769 to 1782 established a string of California missions, were to little avail. Charles III ended up losing Florida and Belice to the British. His son, Charles IV, not only transferred Oregon, Washington, and Vancouver Island to the British, but also ceded the vast Louisiana territory to France.

The Bourbon economic reforms did increase commerce and mining, strengthening the criollo business sector and staving off royal treasury bankruptcy. But it was the imposition of the reforms, along with the increased colonial militarization and the Jesuits' expulsion, that made clear to all the monarchy's absolutist bent. While the church hierarchy supported the Crown, Bourbon suspicion of church corporate power and a drained royal treasury led Charles IV in 1804 to issue a Cédula Real (royal decree), ordering the sale of church real estate, with the proceeds and all the church's liquid capital payable as a forced loan to finance Crown expenditures. Since the church was the principal lender for criollo business ventures, the effect of withdrawing its capital from the private credit market threw the colonial economy into chaos and provoked vehement opposition.

When in 1808 Napoleon Bonaparte forced the abdication of Ferdinand VII, placing José Bonaparte on the Spanish throne, shocked colonials made several unsuccessful attempts to break with the usurpers and form a local government loyal to the imprisoned Bourbon monarch. In virtually every attempt, the hierarchy maneuvered behind the scenes, and after one failed plot Mercedarian Father Melchor de Talamantes died in the dungeons of San Juan de Ulúa prison for his conspiratorial role. To appease the hierarchy, the Cédula Real was repealed in 1809, and Archbishop Francisco Javier de Lizana y Beaumont was named the Bonapartist viceroy. But diocesan and provincial clergy, who had assumed the Jesuits' sympathy toward the grievances of the colonials, were not so easily assuaged.

Independence

In September 1810, a conspiracy between pro-Bourbon military officers and members of the clergy in Querétaro and Guanajuato was uncovered. Warned of their impending arrest, the conspirators hastened to act, and before dawn on Sunday, September 16, in the town of Dolores, Father Miguel Hidalgo rallied his indigenous and mestizo parishioners to a call for independence. Hidalgo's role in the plot had been to organize the "lower clergy," and eventually some four hundred priests did respond by taking arms in the independence struggle. The hierarchy, on the other hand, saw no benefit in insurrection organized from below and reacted immediately, with Bishop Manuel Abad y Quiepo of Michoacán excommunicating Hidalgo and his fellow conspirators.

The excommunications were insufficient, however, to deter an essentially campesino revolt by indigenous and mestizo rebels, who felt that they, and not the hierarchy, had God on their side. Led by Hidalgo, they marched cross country under the banner of the Virgin of Guadalupe, with "Long Live Religion, Long Live Our Holiest Mother of Guadalupe" among their slogans. The Indians' participation was rooted in what has been termed a "radical millenarianism,"[15] based on the hope that in defeating the Spaniards they could return to their ancestral ways and reclaim their collective rights to their long-lost lands. The idea of indigenous hordes on the rampage repelled many criollos, who preferred to side for the moment with the peninsulares. Seeing that for the largely indigenous masses the Virgin had become an "inspirational symbol of social justice and land distribution,"[16] the peninsulares countered by sending troops into battle under the banner of Spain's own Virgen de los Remedios.

Hidalgo's lack of military training was shown by his inability to control the undisciplined troops, whose hatred for their peninsular and criollo masters had been seething for centuries. The first rebel victories were consequently marred by pillage, summary executions, and massacres of civilians. Serious rebel defeats followed, and Hidalgo was captured in 1811 and executed. The movement was kept alive by mestizo Father José María Morelos, a former seminary student of Hidalgo, who gave the rebellion political substance with a series of manifestos that melded sympathy for the Indians with progressive European ideals. Upon his capture and execution in 1815, the movement all but disappeared except for isolated guerrilla movements led by die-hard insurgents.

In fact, it was the church hierarchy's reaction to European events that ultimately determined Mexico's independence. Under Bonaparte, the radical ideals of the French Revolution had spread to Spain. New democratic reforms in 1812 abolished the Inquisition and affected the religious orders' and the hierarchy's privileges. Spain's parliament, known as the *cortes*, and its democratic constitution were suppressed when Fernando VII returned to power in 1814. But they were brought back in 1820, when mutinous troops demanded the constitution's reinstatement as a condition for Fernando's continuance in power. Fearful of losing privilege and wealth, the colonial church hierarchy adroitly decided independence was more desirable. Plotting with disaffected criollos, they financed a military commander of dubious repute, Agustín de Iturbide, who in early 1821 turned his troops against the Crown and declared Mexico a constitutional monarchy. Military victory came within months, and upon independence an interim regency offered Mexico's throne to Fernando VII, the state religion became Catholicism, and the criollo ideal of equality among citizens seemed guaranteed.

In a twist of fate, however, the *cortes* prohibited Ferdinand from accepting

Mexico's crown, prompting Iturbide's brief reign as "Emperor" in 1822–23. A constituent assembly in 1824 adopted the U.S. model of federated states and passed Mexico's first constitution, marking the beginning of a tumultuous era. From 1821 to 1871, more than fifty federal governments and thirty different presidents oversaw a period of regional factionalism, economic dislocation, coups, and countercoups at the service of nineteenth-century Liberal and Conservative politicians. Military defeat in the 1846–48 U.S.-Mexican War resulted in the cession of half of Mexico's entire territory to the United States — not to mention jurisdiction over dozens of nomadic indigenous tribes inhabiting those lands.

Church and State

The Catholic Church was also in disarray, with royalist bishops and many members of the colonial clergy either expelled or having fled from independent Mexico. The number of diocesan clergy dropped from 4,229 in 1810 to 3,232 in 1851,[17] and only six religious orders remained in Mexico, while vocations to the priesthood dwindled — leaving vast areas of the countryside virtually churchless. The indigenous population was abandoned to the practice of its own blend of indigenous religiosity, Christian belief, and superstition, while the ruling criollo caste and the increasing number of mestizo Mexicans grappled with an enduring identity crisis: how to be both a "good Catholic" and a "good Mexican" when church hierarchy and government were so often at odds.

First of all, there was the immediate church-state issue of the *patronato real*. With the new government claiming the Spanish Crown's right to make appointments to vacant church positions, the Mexican hierarchy decided the *patronato* no longer existed and told the government to seek Vatican permission for any appointments. For its part, the Vatican refused until 1836 to even recognize the government's existence. Within this vacuum, church-state relations were complicated, first, by the hierarchy's claim to its traditional diezmo tithe, and then the confiscation of minor church properties by several federal administrations and by claims of various Mexican state governments to jurisdiction in church-related matters.

The hierarchy clearly had less to fear from the Conservatives, who were central-government advocates and had inherited many old attitudes of the peninsulares and royalists. The cornerstone of Liberal beliefs, held by mostly provincial politicians who favored decentralized rule, was the ideal of the individual landholder-citizen. The Liberals were not anti-church per se, with many Liberal politicians confessed Catholics. But they did see corporate power such as that held by the church as anathema to modern progress. A taste of what the hierarchy could expect came in 1833, when Liberal legislators angered by the hierarchy's apparent support for Conservatives enacted anti-clerical measures, including prohibition of political criticism from the pulpit, secularization of education, and the rejection of the longstanding practice of government collection of church tithes.

Catholic prelates protested publicly, the Liberal government deported one bishop and ousted others, and the situation was only defused when the president, General Antonio López de Santa Anna, dissolved congress in 1834. To protect traditional military and church privileges, known as *fueros*, Santa Anna arranged a church-state alliance that effectively closed the Liberals out of power for most of twenty years. When Liberals made a political comeback, they legislated the constitution of 1857, which removed Catholicism's privileged position as sole religion, secularized education, and banned the acquisition of property by religious entities. After Pope Pius IX declared the constitution null and void and the bishops denied the sacraments to Liberals sworn to uphold the constitution, a three-year civil war ensued, during which all church properties were expropriated. Only with the triumph in 1861 of Liberal President Benito Juárez, a full-blooded Zapotec Indian, could the new constitution be enforced.

No sooner had Juárez taken office, however, than a Franco-Anglo-Spanish coalition occupied Veracruz in demand of interest payments on Mexico's skyrocketing foreign debt. British and Spanish troops withdrew after reassurances from Juárez, but Napoleon III left his troops in place and then imposed Hapsburg Archduke Maximilian as Emperor of Mexico. Aided by Conservatives and encouraged by the church hierarchy, the bearded and bespectacled Maximilian arrived in 1864 and soon proved to be more liberal than Mexico's Liberals themselves. He did promise special status for Catholicism, but soon angered bishops and the Vatican alike by refusing to repeal the Liberals' anti-church measures. He alienated Conservatives by preserving the 1857 constitution and offering Juárez a place in his government.

With regard to the 40 percent of the population that was still indigenous, Maximilian was more progressive than either Liberals or Conservatives: while previous nineteenth-century governments had suppressed revolts and continued to sell Indians into slavery, Maximilian supported their communal land claims, instituted an imperial protectorate on their behalf, and banned corporal punishment and debt peonage on haciendas. Following Napoleon III's withdrawal of French troops from Mexico, Maximilian, having alienated virtually every power group, was captured and executed by Liberal forces in 1867.

Upon Juárez's death in 1872, the Liberals incorporated the various "Reform Laws" of 1833–61 into the constitution, among them the Ley Lerdo of 1856. Directed at the church, its promotion of individual property ownership and ban on corporate landholding effectively denied recognition of indigenous communal land rights. It was in a way the legal reaffirmation of the same criollo disdain for the Indian that led to rejection of the early independence struggle under Hidalgo. Non-indigenous Mexicans became the nineteenth-century heirs both to the criollos' claim upon the Virgin of Guadalupe as their symbol and to an identity rooted in the ideal of equal rights for the individual under the law. This new Mexican ruling class simply imposed their individualist ideal on the indigenous population, both from a racist belief in their own superiority and from a keen sense of economic expediency. The latter became evident later with the 1883 law on *terrenos baldíos*, which under the pretext of utilizing allegedly abandoned property was used to confiscate vast amounts of communal Indian lands.

The Porfiriato

In 1876, the Liberals lost power in a military coup staged by General Porfirio Díaz, an unruly mestizo politician and free-thinking Mason from Oaxaca state. Díaz ruled Mexico for the next thirty-four years in a personalist dictatorship known as the Porfiriato, in which elections came to be an exercise in high farce. As Porfirio Díaz consolidated his regime, he fostered a new *modus vivendi* with the Catholic Church, at the same time leaving in place a veritable sword of Damocles over the church's head: the Liberal constitution of 1857. While refusing to repeal the constitution, Díaz also continued the Liberals' encouragement of the evangelization of Mexico by U.S. Protestant mission societies.

From 1871, U.S. mainstream Protestant missionaries had begun arriving, the Quakers appearing first, followed within a decade by Presbyterians, Congregationalists, Methodists, and Baptists.[18] Buying up Catholic church properties confiscated by the Liberal Lerdo de Tejada government, the Protestant missionaries prospered, especially among those sectors of the populace that saw Catholicism as an obstacle to modern progress. With their numbers growing rapidly around Mexico City, along the northern border, and among campesinos, miners, and workers in Chihuahua, Zacatecas, and Monterrey, the Protestants focused their attention on building churches and schools and publishing religious tracts. From 1877 to 1882 alone, the number of Protestant congregations in Mexico nearly doubled from 125 to 239 and by 1890 grew by another 137 percent to a total of 566.[19] While total numbers were small, the Protestant churches continued to expand throughout the Porfiriato, especially along Mexico's Gulf coast and in Veracruz, Puebla, and northern Mexico.

Díaz countered the Catholic hierarchy's displeasure by deftly cultivating personal relations with Catholic prelates, most notably Bishop Eulogio Gillow of Oaxaca, whose father, a British businessman, had made the family fortune in Mexico. At the same time, Díaz also ordered his minions to overlook church violations of the constitution. Under such semi-legal circumstances, the buffeted Mexican church began a de facto recovery. From 1878 to 1895 the number of churches nearly doubled to 9,580; Catholic jurisdictions increased dramatically to include seven archdioceses, twenty-three dioceses, and one apostolic vicariate by 1905; the number of diocesan clergy grew by more than 10 percent,[20] Catholic universities were reopened, and twenty-six diocesan seminaries were established nationwide.[21] Religious orders were welcomed back and a virtual second evangelization was begun, with the Franciscans moving further west to Colima and the Jesuits founding missions among Huichol and Cora Indians in Nayarit.

Cordial church-state relations, the solemn coronation of the image of the Virgin of Guadalupe in 1895, and the welcome of a papal envoy in 1896 after thirty-one years without Mexico-Vatican diplomatic ties followed Pope Leo XIII's invitation in 1878 to Díaz and other heads of state for closer collaboration with Catholic officials.[22] But what Díaz could not have immediately foreseen was the criticism of his regime that would be engendered by Leo XIII's social encyclical *Rerum Novarum* (1891). By 1890, the economic policies of the *científicos*, a group of young technocratic advisors to Díaz, was moving Mexico's stagnant agrarian economy toward increased commerce, mining of industrial metals, and manufacturing for export. The Díaz regime lowered tariffs and trade barriers, opened the economy to foreign investment, encouraged European immigration, built railroads, strung telephone lines, and sent factory output soaring. Huge fortunes were made by Mexican and foreign investors, with the *científicos* benefitting handsomely through influence peddling all the while.

But those who worked in the factories were certainly not sharing in the fruits of their labor, as *Rerum Novarum* had suggested they should. Excessively low wages were virtually frozen in the years 1877–1900, and those who dared strike for better conditions met with violent repression from the army and police. Conditions were even worse in the countryside, inhabited by 70 percent of all Mexicans. Despite a population increase of 50 percent since 1877, more than 97 percent of heads of rural households in half a dozen states had no land to work in 1910.[23] Nationwide, the average daily wage for farm laborers dropped by nearly 24 percent during the same period[24] as the Díaz regime emphasized agricultural production for export.

When henequen planters required a virtual slave work force, Díaz amicably responded with the forced relocation of thousands of Yaqui Indian prisoners from Sonora to work on plantations in Oaxaca and Yucatán. With food production virtually abandoned, the result was rural starvation; streams of landless campesinos migrated to urban and mining centers, providing a ready source of cheap labor.

A growing number of Mexican Protestant pastors and schoolteachers, many with links to Masonic lodges and Liberal circles, were taking an increasingly active part in protests and demonstrations over the Díaz economic policies and lack of political freedom.[25] The Catholic hierarchy, meanwhile, largely ignored the inequities of the system, wishing above all to foster respect for authority and appease that "superior man who governs us,"[26] as Ignacio Montes de Oca, bishop of San Luis Potosí, referred to Díaz in 1900. There were occasional exceptions: Bishop Ramón Camacho García of Querétaro issued pastoral letters criticizing both the excesses of usury and the exploitation of indebted peons on the haciendas,[27] while Bishop Francisco Orozco of Chiapas was derisively nicknamed "Chamula" by a local elite who loathed him for criticizing the brutal repression of rebellious Tzotzil Indians, descendants of those same Indians defeated by the Spaniards at Chamula in 1524.[28]

But it was largely left to the Catholic religious orders, diocesan clergy, and laity outraged by growing social inequities to act upon the ideas put forward in *Rerum Novarum*. The resultant movement of "Social Catholicism," although pro-hierarchy and pro-papacy, nevertheless countered the economic injustices with the offer of social and political action based upon Catholic sociology. As an alternative solution to "Masonic liberalism" and European socialism, the movement surfaced in Mexico around 1895 in nascent Catholic labor groups called "Catholic Circles," most notably the "Catholic Workers of Guadalajara" organized by diocesan and Jesuit priests. The movement spread and in 1903 won sufficient hierarchy support to be able to hold the first of several church congresses on social issues.

Formation of the first campesino group of Operarios Guadalupanos in Hidalgo state followed in 1905, and the rural labor movement spread rapidly, with the help of lay activist José Refugio Galinda, the "apostle of Catholic agrarianism."[29] In 1908, Father José María Troncoso, Mexican Josephite provincial superior, established the Catholic Workers Union to unite the dispersed Catholic labor circles. In October 1910, as a revolt against Díaz was brewing, one of the few prelates to promote the Catholic labor movement, Archbishop José Mora y del Río of Mexico City, inaugurated a week-long national conference of the Operarios Guadalupanos, who had become sharply critical of the government in demanding better wages and decent housing for farm laborers.

The Revolution

The majority of bishops nevertheless kept their distance from the Social Catholic movement, especially as Díaz came under increasing political pressure. When the dictator had himself re-elected once again in 1910, a jailed political opponent, Francisco I. Madero, escaped to Texas, where he declared a revolt based upon the principles of "Effective Suffrage" and "No Re-election." It marked the start of a period of political turmoil and civil war that has gone down in history as the Mexican Revolution. The decadent Díaz regime literally collapsed within months as federal troops failed to contain armed movements led by Emiliano Zapata in the south and various rebel leaders in the north, including the bandit-turned-revolutionary Pancho Villa. As the octogenarian dictator resigned and fled the country in May 1911, Catholic social activists got the hierarchy's approval to move into the political arena and founded the National Catholic Party (PCN).

In line with Vatican advice against supporting anti-Díaz forces,[30] many Mexican bishops were openly antagonistic to Madero, a wealthy, U.S.-educated Catholic from northern Mexico who dabbled in spiritism. Still, his widespread support among lay Catholics and the lower clergy prompted the PCN to join in nominating him as candidate for the presidential election of October 1911. Madero won easily, and the Catholic party began organizing for the June 1912 national elections, in which it scored impressive victories: it won nearly 30 percent of the lower house of the federal congress and four senate seats, four state governorships, all the seats in the Jalisco state congress, clear majorities in four other state legislatures,[31] and scores of mayoral and municipal council elections, most notably in the major cities of Puebla and Toluca.[32]

Madero meanwhile proved to be a weak president, and his reticence to enact sweeping land reforms prompted Zapatista rebels to again take up arms. In effect, the Mexican Revolution was in many ways a replay of the independence struggle: indigenous and mestizo rebels hoping for radical change saw their movement diverted by a criollo caste seeking to protect its own economic and political interests. And, as had happened then, the first to take up arms once again marched into battle wearing emblems of the Virgin of Guadalupe.

But there was one significant difference between the rebel movements of 1810 and 1910: by the time Emiliano Zapata and his followers issued their Plan of Ayala manifesto in 1911, Mexico's ethnic and social makeup had undergone a remarkable transformation. Nearly 80 percent of the country's 15 million people still lived in the countryside, but official census figures show a key change: in the century since independence, Mexico's indigenous peoples had declined from 55 percent of the population to just under 40 percent. The decrease actually may not have been as great as that, given Mexican Indians' demonstrated reticence in modern times to acknowledge their ethnicity — an attempt to pass as mestizos to avoid ingrained racial and cultural discrimination in Mexico. Still, there is no doubt that the mixed-blood mestizo caste had grown steadily since the Spanish conquistador Cortés sired his first offspring with the Coatzacoalcan Nahuatl-speaking Indian princess known as "La Malinche." Occupying the social notch above the indigenous population, during the nineteenth century mestizos advanced as small farmers, ranchers, teachers, and bureaucrats, becoming the dominant segment of the population by 1910.

Emiliano Zapata was a product of that mestizo class, though still close to his indigenous roots in Anenecuilco, a village in Morelos state whose lands had been absorbed into the local hacienda. A moderately prosperous sharecropper, handsome and mustachioed — and a bit of a provincial dandy in his broad-brimmed *charro* hat — Zapata was admired by wealthy hacendados far and wide for his horse-wrangling skills. Nevertheless, he was acutely aware of their condescension towards him as a mestizo and chafed under the classist and cultural discrimination that he faced. As such, his sympathies turned toward underprivileged small farmers, who in 1909 chose him as Anenecuilco village president.

Unable to recuperate stolen communal lands, paid the equivalent of just 12.5 U.S. cents per day as hacienda laborers,[33] indebted through forced purchases at the *tiendas de raya,* the stores on the haciendas, villagers and landless peons throughout Morelos rallied behind Zapata during the Madero-inspired revolt that drove Díaz from power. But once in power, the slight and serious Madero, a product of the wealthy northern hacienda class, appeared interested only in paying lip service to agrarian reform. Frustrated and impatient, in late 1911 Zapata and his followers rebelled against Madero, issuing their militant Plan of Ayala manifesto, which proclaimed their movement to be national in scope and called for widespread land redistribution.

Constitutionalists and Zapatistas

In 1913 General Victoriano Huerta engineered a vile palace coup with the support of the U.S. embassy, murdering Madero, his brother, and his vice-president. Upon declaring himself president, Huerta offered the PCN the possibility of forming a ruling congressional coalition — an offer rejected by the Catholic party. But the hierarchy's desire to accommodate the church to whomever held power kept it from condemning Huerta, thereby effectively extending de facto recognition to him, a move that proved to be a costly political mistake. The bishops further admonished the PCN leadership to quell its anti-Huerta feelings, reminding them of the church's censure of rebellion against civil authority. Others were not so cautious, however. The governor of northern Coahuila state, Venustiano Carranza, launched a "Constitutionalist" revolt against the usurper Huerta, which also served to undercut the Zapatistas' agrarian reform–based rebel movement.

As the chasm between the Constitutionalists and Zapatistas widened, so did their divergence in how they addressed the question of religion and the Catholic Church. As did Hidalgo and Morelos in the independence struggle, Zapata managed to rally the lower clergy and devout mestizo and indigenous peasants to his cause. Indeed, in 1914, when Zapatista brigades triumphantly entered Mexico City bearing the Virgin of Guadalupe's standard, they were greeted with the welcoming peal of church bells.[34] That is not to say that the Zapatista movement was exclusively Catholic: in Morelos, Puebla, and Oaxaca, rural Methodist ministers were particularly effective in rallying impoverished campesinos to the cause.[35] But the majority of the Zapatista rank and file were certainly Catholic, which translated into considerable church backing for the rebels.

Among Zapatista supporters were several priests, including the parish priest of Huautla, who is believed to have typed up the Plan of Ayala on his own typewriter. Zapata's stunning white stallion was a gift from the parish pastor of Axochiapan, and one priest is believed to have risen to the rank of colonel in the Zapatista army.[36] While the Catholic hierarchy could not bring itself to support rebellion against authority and most prelates had fled the country by 1914, Bishop Manuel Fulcheri Pietrasanta of Cuernavaca was an exception.[37] He remained in his Zapatista-controlled diocese, was allowed to make pastoral rounds, attempted to mediate a truce, and later acknowledged that the rebels' "Christian sentiments, and particularly [their] respect for things sacred, have deeper roots than one might believe at first glance."[38]

Likewise, in Jalisco state, Archbishop Francisco Orozco of Guadalajara — the former Chiapas bishop whose support for Indians had angered Porfirian authorities — went into hiding among campesinos after being charged by the Constitutionalists with sedition and conspiracy. Orozco reappeared only when Pancho Villa's troops "liberated"[39] Guadalajara in December 1914 from anti-church terror. In fact, Carranza's Constitutionalists hoped to punish the church for failing to condemn Huerta and not backing their rebellion: in areas under their control, the Constitutionalists closed seminaries and schools, fined, jailed, and executed priests, raped nuns, pillaged and burned churches, and destroyed the statues of village saints.

The followers of Pancho Villa, on the other hand, showed themselves more akin to the Zapatistas as regards the church. After breaking with Carranza in 1914, the paunchy brigand-turned-brigadier wrested most of west-central Mexico from Carrancista control. In Michoacán, Jalisco, Colima, and Zacatecas, Catholics in open revolt against the Constitutionalists joined Villa's forces, with one Catholic priest becoming a Villista general.[40] Church bells rang out as Villa's troops entered Morelia, and in Guadalajara the Villistas freed jailed clergy and reopened churches. Villa was sharply critical of Carranza, saying he had "destroyed freedom of conscience . . . and profoundly offended the religious sentiments of the people."[41]

The light-skinned, bearded, and bespectacled Carranza was an avatar of the old criollo caste that had recoiled from radical change a century earlier. A wealthy hacienda owner and Porfirian politician who backed Madero in 1910, Carranza offered no immediate program for social change, seducing Villa and other northern leaders — Protestant and Catholic, many with Liberal, labor, and anarcho-syndicalist pasts — to join his political revolt. Alvaro Obregón, a former hacienda foreman and teacher from Sonora, was a Constitutionalist stalwart, as was Plutarco Elías Calles, a fellow Sonoran, teacher, and failed bureaucrat.

Carranza's was a coalition of large landholders and the emerging urban classes, which at the time accounted for less than a quarter of Mexico's population. They preferred moderate land reform, with haciendas and small private landholdings coexisting as an alternative to the radical Zapatista demands. Many of them viewed the campesino religiosity and almost mystical ties to the land as retrograde; and, as heirs to the Bourbons and nineteenth-century Liberals, they were profoundly mistrustful of Catholicism's corporate power.

With Villa and Zapata unable to maintain unity, the Constitutionalists isolated the Zapatistas in Morelos; then Obregón roundly defeated Villa, making the Constitutionalists the dominant faction by 1916. Carranza wanted a new constitution to grant sweeping presidential powers that he hoped would restore order to Mexico, and so he called a constitutional convention, decreeing a law that barred as delegates anyone who had fought against the Constitutionalists, as well as any political party representing specific religions or ethnic groups. Villistas, Zapatistas, and the National Catholic Party — not to mention direct representatives of indigenous groups, which accounted for nearly 40 percent of the population — were thus excluded from the convention that drafted the constitution of 1917, which has governed Mexico ever since.[42]

The new constitution was the work of a coalition of large landholders, military chieftains, urban labor unionists, and liberal Jacobin intellectuals. It surpassed Carranza's own desires for moderate land reform, assimilating

Zapatista demands for mandating expropriation and redistribution of large landholdings. It also incorporated earlier calls by labor unions and Catholic workers' circles for improved working conditions and wages. The Constitutionalists had never forgiven the Catholic hierarchy for its failure to condemn Huerta and support the Carranza revolt, and the majority Jacobin and anarcho-syndicalist convention delegates made nineteenth-century Reform Laws look mild compared to anti-clerical measures in the new constitution: Article 3 forbade religious education; Article 5 banned monastic orders; Article 24 forbade open-air church services; Article 27 effectively expropriated all churches by prohibiting religious ownership of real estate; and, to prevent court challenges, Article 130 denied "any legal capacity whatsoever [to] the religious groupings known as churches."

The majority of the hierarchy, exiled in the United States, immediately issued a pastoral letter with papal approval protesting that the new constitution violated the inalienable rights of the church, society, and individuals, and complaining that it revoked what legal recognition the church had enjoyed under the 1857 constitution. The government's resolve to enforce the anti-church legislation measures was immediately tested. Following Carranza's May 1917 inauguration as president, Guadalajara's Archbishop Orozco, who had returned from exile in the United States and again gone into hiding, issued a pastoral letter mildly critical of the government, which was read from pulpits throughout the archdiocese. The Constitutionalist government countered by closing the churches where the letter had been read, and in 1918 the Jalisco legislature cracked down with a limit on the number of priests allowed in the state. Guadalajara erupted in street demonstrations, the church suspended liturgical services, and a Catholic boycott paralyzed the city. The authorities soon relented, but the incident was indicative of what was soon to come.

3

From Cristo Rey to Tlatelolco

A FTER PRESIDING over the assassination of Emiliano Zapata in April 1919, Venustiano Carranza was himself murdered the following year by troops partisan to Alvaro Obregón — who, after a brief interim government, became Mexico's president in 1920. With Obregón occupied in trying to consolidate his government, the federal administration looked the other way as the church hierarchy ignored the constitutional limits on its activities. Believing church persecution to be caused by religious ignorance, the bishops concentrated on a renewed campaign of evangelization. By 1925, five new dioceses had been created, missionary activities expanded, and religious orders, particularly congregations of women, grew at a rapid rate.[1] Education continued in semi-clandestine Catholic schools, and adult participation in lay organizations was promoted. The hierarchy created the Mexican Social Secretariat (SSM) in 1920 to coordinate the mushrooming Catholic associations, and during the next five years scores of week-long Semana Social conferences for discussion of social issues were held nationwide. In practical terms, it was a revival of Social Catholicism — albeit bereft of the PCN — aimed at competing for adherents with the Mexican church's now rather concrete enemies of socialism and Masonic liberalism.

Despite the lax enforcement of constitutional anti-church proscriptions under Obregón, the Catholic hierarchy was concerned over close ties between many government officials and leftist political parties, labor unions, and anti-clerical associations. The recruitment of Mexican Communist Party (PCM) artists and intellectuals by Secretary of Education José Vasconcelos for his post-revolutionary "cultural renaissance," the growing influence of the Mexican Anti-Clerical Federation, the brief socialist experiment begun in the Yucatán by ex-Zapatista Felipe Carrillo Puerto, and the ruthless statewide church persecution in Tabasco by Governor Tomás Garrido Canabal — all were worrisome signs for Catholic bishops.

Furthermore, the hierarchy blanched at the anti-Catholic bent of Vasconcelos's headlong plunge into the church's centuries-old domain of education. Only 34 percent of Mexicans were literate in 1921, prompting Vasconcelos to launch a massive teacher-training and alphabetization campaign, especially in rural areas. Many rural teachers had scant education themselves, most blamed Catholic education or lack of it for rural underdevelopment, many were socialists, and even more were Protestants. In fact, not only were post-revolution administrations looking favorably at Jewish immigration to Mexico,[2] but the inroads being made by liberal-minded Protestants into the Education Secretariat and government in general were of serious concern to the Catholic hierarchy.

Scores of rural Protestant pastors, school teachers, and liberal urban businessmen — Methodists in Puebla and Morelos, Evangelicals and Congregationalists in Chihuahua, Presbyterians throughout the north and in Tabasco — had been key activists during Madero's "anti-reelectionist" movement and in the armed rebellion that drove Díaz from power.[3] Sponsored by Carranza and Obregón, many now entered the post-revolutionary federal bureaucracy, beginning a notable tradition of Protestant influence in public education. Indicative was the rise of Episcopalian Bishop Moisés Sáenz Garza from public education director in 1915, to director of the National Preparatory School in 1919, to *Oficial Mayor*, undersecretary, and finally head of the Education Secretariat.[4]

Following the divisive revolution, the ideology behind Vasconcelos's educational and cultural "renaissance" was based upon a need for a common identity to unite the "many Mexicos" — cultural and geographic — that existed within the same nation. The education secretary found that ideology expressed in the writings of anthropologist Manuel Gamio and others, particularly in Gamio's 1916 book, *Forjando Patria* (Forging a Fatherland). *Indigenismo*, as the ideology was called, promoted incorporation of "positive" aspects of indigenous culture and of the Indians themselves into Mexican national life. The movement tended toward the folkloric, with a romanticized vision of history, and those who fell under its spell claimed the equal influence of conquerors and conquered upon each other — even "to the extent that one can speak about mixture of culture as well as blood."[5] Turning a blind eye to discrimination, they fallaciously posited that Mexicans of all races and cultures were now able to compete in all fields under "equal circumstances."[6]

It was, obviously, a myth: although mestizos were now the preponderant racial group, the culture that dominated was, and since 1521 had been, European and Hispanic. In fact, Indian children in rural schools nationwide were taught the values of Mexican nationalism exclusively in a European language, Spanish. In Mexico City's Casa del Estudiante Indígena, boys aged twelve to fifteen were taken "from the heart of tribal life, to be taught Spanish [and] modern Mexican ways"[7] — and then reinserted into their communities as agents of change. The true goal was clearly the "continuance of mestizos as the predominant ethnic group and as the leading political class of the population."[8] Critics have since recognized *indigenismo* as a romantic continuation of the "de-Indianization"[9] of Mexico's native peoples begun four centuries earlier.

The Cristeros

While church-state tensions over education existed, they were mild compared to the rupture that began in February 1921 with a bomb blast at the Mexico City archdiocesan curia. Another bomb in November in the Basilica of Guadalupe provoked Catholic outcry and the formation of a Catholic "National Guard" to protect the Virgin's image on display there. In 1923, the Vatican delegate, Archbishop Ernesto Filippi, was deported for technical violation of the constitution by participating in an open-air Mass held to dedicate a monument to *Cristo Rey*, Christ the King. Then in October 1924 the government-allied CROM labor federation violently broke up a national eucharistic congress, causing a major rift in church-state relations.

That same month, Plutarco Elías Calles became president as Obregón temporarily retired to Sonora, where he proceeded to appropriate lands belonging to the Yaqui Indians. With church persecution continuing unabated in Jalisco and Tabasco, Calles ordered increased vigilance of the church nationwide as anti-clerical radicals promoted a schismatic Mexican Apostolic Catholic Church. Angry campesinos began to stockpile arms and urban Catholics formed the National League for the Defense of Religious Freedom. In February 1926, Calles reacted to a sensationalist news story reiterating the hierarchy's censure of the constitution with deportation of foreign priests and nuns, closure of Catholic schools and monasteries, and moves to enforce constitutional anti-church measures. Priests were required to register with state governments, another Vatican delegate was expelled, and just as the "Calles Law" establishing penal regulation of Article 130 was set to take effect, the hierarchy struck back on July 31 with suspension of liturgical services nationwide.

The move sparked the Cristero rebellion (1926–29), an uprising often depicted as wholly religious and "led by priests" who manipulated "illiterate, conservative peasants."[10] In fact, mestizo and indigenous campesinos — many of them former Villistas and Zapatistas — unearthed their weapons and took to the hills to continue the revolutionary struggle against what they perceived as the *mal gobierno* (bad government). Caught off guard, the hierarchy actually denounced the armed struggle and most priests in the rural conflict zones abandoned their parishes. Only forty priests were known to be actively pro-Cristero, and just five ever served in combat roles.[11] From their U.S. exile, the hierarchy attempted to harness the movement, as did the urban-based Religious Freedom League, whose activists botched a bombing attempt on Obregón's life in 1927 — for which Jesuit Father Miguel A. Pro Juárez was framed and executed by firing squad. In 1928, a League member did manage to assassinate the ex-president before he was able to take office for a second term.

The hierarchy, the League, and the Cristeros were worlds apart, however. In the countryside, the land question was equally as important to the uprising as religion. With agrarian reform proceeding slowly, ex-hacienda peons and indigenous communities were largely without the collective ejido land titles promised in 1917. Strife resulted between campesinos who had been granted land and those who had not. First Obregón and then Calles armed and employed mostly landless rural peasants called *agraristas* as shock troops against campesinos with legitimate claims.[12] The Catholic hierarchy and some priests complicated things, sending mixed signals as to the morality of accepting expropriated private property. But it was a volatile mix that ignited rural Mexico — both corruption and violence, along with a threatened end to land reform and unwanted government intrusion into village life that revolved around religious fiestas and ancient reverence for patron deities-turned-saints.[13]

To the battle cry of *Viva Cristo Rey y Santa María de Guadalupe!* former Villistas and Zapatistas took up arms from Zacatecas and Aguascalientes in the north to Morelos and Guerrero in the south.[14] In 1927, the League hired a former revolutionary general to assume military command, and by 1929 there were twenty-five thousand armed rebels in the field and an estimated twenty-five thousand in reserve.[15] The growing autonomy of both the Cristeros and the League divided the hierarchy. Prelates such as Archbishop Orozco extended tacit support, while Archbishop Leopoldo Ruiz y Flores of Morelia and Bishop Pascual Díaz of Tabasco secretly advocated a truce.

The Vatican, the U.S. State Department, and the U.S. Catholic hierarchy used Ruiz and Díaz to persuade fellow Mexican bishops meeting in Texas that the war was neither winnable nor in the hierarchy's best interest.[16] Behind the backs of the Cristeros and the League, church-state negotiations were arranged in Mexico City through U.S. Ambassador Dwight D. Morrow, and an "understanding" was reached in June 1929: the hierarchy agreed to rein in the Cristeros and the League, the clergy would resume liturgical services in reopened churches, and the government agreed to take a "flexible" approach to enforcement of the constitution.[17]

League activists were furious at the accords, more so when virtually concurrent with the formation of the Mexican Bishops Conference (CEM) in 1929 Díaz was rewarded by being named archbishop of Mexico City and Ruiz y Flores was appointed Vatican delegate. In February 1930, a fanatical young Catholic shot and wounded President Pascual Ortiz Rubio, one of three interim presidents controlled by Calles after Obregón's assassination in 1928. The government responded with a political crackdown, especially targeting the increasingly militant Communist party. Cristeros who had kept their weapons staged sporadic revolts into 1933, while anti-church attacks continued in Tabasco and elsewhere, and the fragile church-state *modus vivendi* was upset by papal criticism of the government and the expulsion of Bishop Díaz.

The Cárdenas Era

While out of office, Calles had maintained virtual control of the government through the National Revolutionary Party (PNR), formed in 1929 to consolidate the rule of the post-revolutionary regime. Calles was still powerful in 1934 and shocked church sensibilities by openly declaring state control of education to be a necessary step toward complete secularization of society. A subsequent constitutional mandate of sex education and socialist-oriented instruction caused a new church-state clash in 1934, just as General Lázaro Cárdenas became president. In his rise from printer's assistant to president, Cárdenas had fought in the revolution under Calles, helped suppress a Yaqui revolt in Sonora in 1918, battled the Cristeros, and served as governor of Michoacán, as president of the PNR, and as federal Secretary of the Interior and Secretary of Defense. Today he is best remembered for his nationalization of the foreign-owned oil industry and efforts to resolve Mexico's inequitable distribution of land. During his presidency he redistributed more than 42 million acres to landless indigenous and campesino communities — three times more than all his predecessors since 1917.

The Mexican bishops' initial alarm over Cárdenas's personal agnosticism and support of socialist ideals was allayed over time by the president's moderate interpretation of the constitutional amendment on education. Even so, the continuing murders of Cristero leaders and harassment of Catholics by local governments provoked a second Cristero uprising. By the end of 1935 there were seventy-five hundred armed rebels — many of them indigenous — in guerrilla bands in remote areas of fifteen states.[18] The renewed Cristero struggle and rumblings within the military prompted Cárdenas to take steps to placate Catholics. After Cárdenas's break with Calles in 1935, the hierarchy eventually set aside its misgivings over the government's expropriation policies, which effected some church properties. Key bishops even encouraged Catholics to pay their taxes so as to contribute toward paying off a foreign debt swollen by indemnity payments from the petroleum expropriation in 1938.

Meanwhile, political polarization in Europe spawned the formation of Mexico's militant National Sinarquist Union in 1937, modeled after the Spanish Catholic fascist Falange movement. Fanatical urban middle-class leaders and largely campesino bases from the fading Cristero movement were fashioned into a politico-paramilitary organization in the name of "Fatherland, Justice, and Liberty." The bishops eschewed open support of *sinarquismo*, instead employing Mexican Catholic Action (ACM) leaders to try to control it. At the opposite end of the political spectrum, the hierarchy was more concerned with Cárdenas's support for the Communist-dominated Spanish Republican government, infamous for church persecution during Spain's civil war. Still another reason for suspicion was Cárdenas's patronage of the Summer Institute of Linguistics, whose work dovetailed neatly with official *indigenismo*.[19] The SIL undertook the apparently noble work of translating the Bible to teach Indians to read and write in their own languages — always, however, with the intention of converting them to Evangelical Protestantism in the process.

In the end, however, it was Cárdenas's role in cementing the bases of Mexico's modern single-party state that most affected the Catholic Church, providing the first institutional counterpart to church corporative power since colonial times. In 1938, Cárdenas restructured and renamed the PNR the Mexican Revolutionary Party (PRM), with the military, organized labor, campesino unions, and grassroots urban organizations becoming the party's four pillars of political support. Since virtually all government officials at every level were members of the PRM, the party held the reins of state control — including the electoral apparatus — moving Mexico towards what has come to be called a "perfect dictatorship" in the guise of modern democracy.

Thus far, Archbishop Díaz's promotion of Catholic Action along with the coordination of various social Catholic organizations through the Mexican Social Secretariat had been the church response to government hegemony. But in 1939 a group of middle-class Catholic activists joined former members of the semi-independent National Union of Catholic Students to found the conservative National Action Party (PAN) in an attempt to counter the PRM's political prowess. The new party had tacit support from some bishops, but the hierarchy's gaze was directed elsewhere: after the PRM electoral machine gave 94 percent of the presidential vote to General Manuel Avila Camacho in 1940, the hierarchy responded positively to the president-elect's admission that he was a "believer," to his emphasis on family values, and to his lack of antagonism toward private schooling. The state seems to have realized that with 95 percent of Mexicans then at least nominally Catholic, striking an alliance with the hierarchy could only help consolidate its political legitimacy. The bishops warmed to the apparent overtures, promoting "Christian patriotism" in the midst of economic crisis and urging support of Mexico's foreign policy following its declaration of war on Germany in 1942, a move unpopular among a significant pro-German segment of the populace.

Indeed, latent anti-U.S. sentiment within the Mexican hierarchy dates to the World War II period, partly due to the sympathy of some prelates toward Germany, but more a result of the influx of U.S. Protestant missionaries, many of whom had been displaced from Asia by the war.[20] Largely as a result of Evangelical and Pentecostal missionary work, the number of Protestants in Mexico nearly doubled from 178,000 in 1940 to 330,000 by 1950.[21] Although the decentralized Evangelical missions were still relatively few in number, an alarmed Catholic hierarchy believed them to be part of a U.S. government plot. Mounting an anti-Protestant campaign, the hierarchy began to identify Catholicism as an "essential element"[22] of Mexican national identity, positing that Protestantism was a beachhead for U.S. domination of the country. Direct criticism of Mexico's principal wartime ally was diverted, however, by a more immediate enemy for the Vatican and Mexican bishops as the war wound down — international Communism.

Post-war Mexico

In the 1946 presidential race, the specter of the Cold War overshadowed Mexican politics. Convinced that the gains of the revolution had been "consolidated," President Avila Camacho rebaptized the official party the Institutional Revolutionary Party (PRI), removed the military as one of the corporate pillars, and hand-picked Interior Secretary Miguel Alemán as his successor. Alemán reportedly had promised to exclude leftists from his government in order to ensure U.S. support for his candidacy. After overcoming a strong opposition challenge with 74 percent of the vote, Alemán became Mexico's first post-revolutionary civilian president. He cut his ties to leftists and initiated an industrial modernization program, pleasing Catholic bishops with its emphasis on private initiative and individual freedoms.

The post-war boom and Alemán's economic policies led to the so-called Mexican miracle, which saw Mexico's gross national product and U.S. investment both jump some 50 percent from 1946 to 1952. Industrial concerns prevailed over agrarian reform: between them, Avila Camacho and Alemán distributed just a quarter of the amount of land portioned out to campesinos by Cárdenas. With large estates increasingly protected from expropriation by court order and with government promotion of smaller *minifundio* private landholdings, there was a significant drop in the percentage of arable land available to communal ejidos. The push factor of rural neglect and the pull factor of urban jobs led to the advent of massive rural-to-urban migration. With an average birth rate of 4.5 percent nationwide, Mexico's urban population swelled to 11 million by 1950 — nearly 43 percent of the country's total population of 25.8 million.

Fifteen years later, more than 55 percent of all Mexicans lived in urban areas, many in squalid shantytowns like those that mushroomed around Mexico City, where the population soared from 1.5 million in 1940 to 8.3 million in 1970. The two decades of post-war industrialization and urbanization dealt a particularly insidious blow to the indigenous roots of Mexican identity. Indians from Chihuahua to Chiapas came under cultural assault as modern roads and telecommunications reached into their remote communities. Rural neglect forced them to leave their communities for Spanish-speaking mestizo villages and towns, where their languages and culture began to disappear. By 1965 only 10 percent of Mexico's 43 million people were still considered culturally indigenous. The urbanization process also saw mestizo farmers and villagers leave for provincial cities or to Texas and California as *bracero* farmworkers, usually trading in their rural lifestyles for the allures of modern urban consumerism. Likewise, provincial urbanites sought work in booming regional centers like Monterrey and Guadalajara or in the capital, Mexico City.

But the resistance to integration displayed by indigenous Mexico throughout the centuries showed itself even in the new urbanization process. The poorest of the migrants, noted one astute observer, were "people who participate in, but who ... do not belong to the urban world."[23] Virtually expelled from a countryside bereft of government support, migrants worked in factories or service jobs while trying to recreate their rural world by growing maize in tiny front yards raising pigs and chickens — sometimes on the roof of their brick or cement-block home! Most retained the religious customs of rural and indigenous Mexico, celebrating their old village festivals in alien surroundings — and invariably making an annual pilgrimage to the Basilica of the Virgin of Guadalupe.

In the midst of the generalized cultural upheaval and degrading poverty, however, some of those marginalized from the benefits of the "Mexican miracle" found in Evangelical Protestantism an "ideology of salvation."[24] In 1940, upon the arrival of the Lutheran Church, the majority of the country's 178,000 Protestants still belonged to "mainstream" denominations that had shed their U.S. origins and become Mexican churches in their own right. But proselytism by "fundamentalist" or Evangelical preachers led to a tripling of the number of Protestants by 1960. After the arrival of Pentecostal churches in the 1920s, the Evangelical churches' growth was stimulated from 1930 to 1950 by a wave of U.S. missionaries and then by itinerant Mexican preachers, many ex-*bracero* farmworkers who had experienced a conversion in the United States before returning to Mexico. In suburban slums and rural areas from which urban migrants originated, congregations such as the Assemblies of God and the Light of the World were increasingly blessed with converts.[25]

While the vast majority of Mexicans adhered to the de facto national religion, Catholicism, others found in their very conversion to Evangelical Protestantism an outlet for their latent "protest" against a system that rejected them.[26] In the countryside, especially in indigenous communities, many village shamans, or *curanderos*, made the obvious transition to becoming faith-healing Pentecostal ministers.[27] Conversion also activated dormant dissent against village *caciques* who exercised economic and political control, often holding monopolies on goods used in festivals honoring Catholic patron saints. Perhaps the most notable such case was in Bishop Samuel Ruiz's diocese in Chiapas, where in 1966 Tzotzil Chamulan *caciques* began expelling poor Evangelical Presbyterian and Seventh-day Adventist villagers who refused to go into debt through obligatory contributions toward the purchase of alcohol, fireworks, and candles for raucous religious festivals.

Catholic officials and the Mexican press had for years railed against the Evangelicals as part of an alleged U.S. plot to extend economic domination and introducing "the American way of life," focusing on groups like the Summer Language Institute or the Mormons to prove their point. But their protests ignored the fact that the vast majority of Evangelical churches were small Mexican congregations, by nature anarchic and detached from national or international superstructures. It also avoided addressing shortcomings in Catholic evangelization that left a vacuum readily filled by the Evangelicals.

The Church and Urbanization

The unwieldy Catholic parish unit — a holdover from medieval Europe, which in modern Mexico was densely populated in urban areas and covered dauntingly expansive areas in the countryside — stifled direct participation of Mexican Catholics in the practice of their faith, as did the liturgy conducted in Latin until 1965. Further, the relative lack of priestly vocations in a church stressing the priest as intermediary between believer and God was a clear problem. The number of diocesan priests was rising, but with rapid population growth there was but one priest for every 7,062 Mexicans in 1960; a century earlier, the ratio had been one per 2,475.[28] Understandably, some of those Mexicans who bore the brunt of the country's socio-economic upheaval found smaller Evangelical congregations, intimate Bible study classes, and the possibility of participating in congregational "meetings" when moved by the Spirit more meaningful than traditional Catholicism.

As the cities grew, Mexico's private sector became vibrant and prosperous, with manufacturing profits increasing more than 800 percent during the 1940s.[29] Alongside the elite of industrialists, a major beneficiary was the new middle class, which replaced the church's troublesome rural constituency as the preferred object of evangelization. The hierarchy set about reorganizing dioceses and establishing new urban parishes. To meet the challenge, it needed to resolve the chronic lack of vocations. Diocesan seminaries were reopened and future seminary rectors — and nearly an entire generation of future Mexican bishops — were schooled with U.S. church support at the Montezuma seminary in New Mexico.

Along with urban parishes, Catholic Action grew in importance as an agent for evangelizing the middle-class. Under the strict control of the bishops, the ACM coordinated a myriad of lay Catholic groups whose activities were doctrinally oriented and largely divorced from the tenets of Social Catholicism. The task of social action was given to the Mexican Social Secretariat, under the gaze of a hierarchy ever-watchful that the church social agency did not cross the line into socialist activism. The SSM organized seminars for Catholic workers and set up and coordinated social assistance centers, shelters, hospices, and dispensaries throughout the republic. In close contact with the urban and rural poor, the SSM and its driving force, Father Pedro Velázquez, soon saw the contradictions in Mexico's economic boom. By 1950, disparities were starkly clear, with 20 percent of the population controlling 60 percent of national wealth, while the poorest 50 percent of Mexicans were left to divide up just 19 percent of the national income.[30]

Institutionally, Catholicism was doing better, but critics have since claimed the gains were made while the hierarchy was engaged in a "mistaken complicity"[31] with the government. The number of dioceses jumped twofold to sixty-four between 1940 and 1970, diocesan priests increased by 50 percent between 1940 and 1960, and the number of priests, brothers, and nuns belonging to religious orders more than doubled between 1950 and 1967.[32] In the face of rampant government corruption, the social problems accompanying urbanization, and political divisions within the ruling PRI, the hierarchy remained virtually silent, however, as President Adolfo

Ruiz Cortines assumed power in 1952 amid serious charges of election fraud.

The church leadership did continue to call for reform of the constitution's anti-church measures during the 1950s. But despite church-state disputes over the content of the PRI government's mandatory school textbooks, and President Adolfo López Mateos's support of Castro in Cuba, the hierarchy opted for a gradual rather than confrontational approach. No longer viewing the regime as the immediate enemy bent on overt secularization of society, the bishops cast about for another foe. They might have found it in growing social inequalities, but when the SSM's Father Velázquez openly criticized the shortcomings of the "Mexican miracle" in 1957, he was silenced by CEM president José Garibi, archbishop of Guadalajara. Instead, the bishops focused on the apparent moral decay of the modern world, launching Catholic Action and associated organizations upon a vigorous national "moralization campaign."[33] Having identified the modern world as the enemy, the hierarchy was kept by the *modus vivendi* with the government from identifying an obvious culprit in moral decay — the government's urban-industrialization program, accompanied by a consumerism that cut at the roots of Mexico's premodern agrarian culture and its spiritual values.

The government's promised continuance of the *modus vivendi* garnered discreet church support for incoming President López Mateos in 1958. But the hierarchy, led by Mexico City's new archbishop, Miguel Darío Miranda, had also begun promoting greater civic action by the laity, resulting in a gradual convergence of interests with the conservative PAN party. The "Mexican miracle" was now tarnished by steady inflation, and the PRI government was increasingly unable to satisfy the growing demands of a population that had doubled since 1930. Private farms using government credits dramatically increased agricultural output for the urban and export markets, while land distribution proceeded at a snail's pace and the growing population of impoverished subsistence farmers was shunted off to the cities and tropical colonization projects. Rural-to-urban migration provided a steady supply of cheap labor, pushing wages below their 1939 levels and generating labor unrest. In 1959 the hierarchy's attention again turned to the Communist threat after a protracted Communist-led railway workers strike and the rise to power of Fidel Castro in Cuba.

Vatican II and a Changing Church

In the early 1960s, the mentality of most Mexican bishops was rooted in the past, the result of a century of church-state struggle and constitutional restrictions. Thus, in 1959 when Pope John XXIII called for a Second Vatican Council to modernize the church, the majority of the Mexican hierarchy was caught off guard — as evidenced by their preparation of an abstract treatise on the spiritual maternity of the Virgin Mary to be presented during the council. Newly named Cardinal Garibi and CEM president José Márquez y Tóriz, archbishop of Puebla, aligned themselves with traditionalists at the council, while Archbishop Miranda took up the hardly novel issue of the lack of vocations in Latin America. The SSM's Father Velázquez attended as an advisor to the bishops on social questions, while younger bishops like Samuel Ruiz of Chiapas, who participated in all four of Vatican II's sessions, observed much while deferring to the church's elder statesmen.

Virtually the only truly "modern" voice among the Mexican prelates as Vatican II began was that of Cuernavaca's Bishop Sergio Méndez Arceo, the fifty-six-year-old nephew of social-action advocate Archbishop José Mora y del Río. An imposing figure — his six-feet-plus frame, bald pate, and horn-rimmed glasses making him a standout in any crowd — Bishop Méndez Arceo provoked outcries in 1958 when he undertook the remodeling of the diocesan cathedral, supplanting the Virgin Mary and a myriad of saints with the Holy Trinity at the center of worship, and replacing traditional organ music with Mexican mariachi groups.[34] In 1960, before Vatican II, he had shown his ecumenical spirit by obtaining John XXIII's permission to distribute less-expensive Protestant editions of the Bible in his diocese in order to make the "good news" available to poor Catholics.[35]

Even as Vatican II was getting underway, Méndez Arceo raised eyebrows by supporting a Freudian psychoanalytical experiment among Benedictines at Our Lady of Resurrection monastery, begun by Belgian Abbot José Gregorio Lemercier with the aim of improving the quality of vocations. Similarly, he backed Austrian theologian and church historian Ivan Illich, who in 1961 established in Cuernavaca one of two Latin American centers to train European and North American missionaries. While the Vatican vetoed continued psychoanalysis among the Benedictines, causing Lemercier and a number of other monks to leave the order, Mexican bishops mounted a successful campaign against Illich's radical ideas on missionary "imperialism" and the need to dismantle church bureaucracy.

Méndez Arceo's was a unique case and caused suspicion among conservative bishops that he would never be able to shake. But much more significant for the Mexican church was the exposure of younger bishops at Vatican II to the climate of new ideas and new approaches to pastoral work and evangelization. In particular, the Vatican II experience led to the formation in 1963 of the Bishops Mutual Aid Union (UMAE), which was the brainchild of Bishop Alfonso Sánchez Tinoco of Papantla. Founded by several prelates from poorer dioceses with the aim of developing a joint pastoral program and coordinating Vatican II reforms, the UMAE experiment was important for several reasons. In immediate terms, the UMAE helped renew the pastorally sclerotic Mexican church by training some twenty-two hundred priests, nuns, and lay Catholics nationwide in its first three years of existence. Also important, in hindsight, were the relationships formed among the young group of bishops. For example, UMAE co-founder Samuel Ruiz placed his thirty-seven-year-old diocesan vicar general and San Cristóbal native, Father Adolfo Suárez Rivera, on the eight-member UMAE national coordinating team. Both had close ties through the UMAE to forty-four-year-old Bishop Ernesto Corripio Ahumada — who in 1952 had become the youngest Catholic prelate in the world when appointed to the diocese of Tampico — that would later play a key role following the Zapatista uprising in 1994.

In the political climate of the early 1960s, the bishops' calls for civic responsibility and political participation and their criticism of official corruption were indirectly benefitting the emerging National Action Party. The PAN's 1964 presidential candidate, ex-Catholic Action leader Jesús González Torres, championed church demands but received a small percentage of ballots cast. The winner was PRI candidate and former Interior Secretary Gustavo Díaz Ordaz, predictably awarded 90 percent of the vote. Following Díaz Ordaz's inauguration and the last session of Vatican II in 1965, both church and state entered a period of crisis.

Annual population growth hovered at about 3.5 percent, nearly matching the annual rate of increase in per capita income and testing the government's ability to meet increased demands on public services. Slowed economic growth prompted frenzied government borrowing, increasing public debt at five times the rate of foreign investment. Díaz Ordaz countered rural population growth, remarkably, by giving out more land than did Cárdenas in the 1930s! But in urban Mexico there were rumblings from the labor sector, while left-leaning students in Morelia, Cuernavaca, and Mexico City were expressing discontent over both a bleak job outlook and scant opportunities for civic participation by non-PRIistas in a one-party state.

At the same time, demands for greater participation also arose within the church after its redefinition at Vatican II of the church as the "people of God" — a non-hierarchical notion that downplayed the institutional bureaucracy and emphasized the importance of the majority of lay Catholics. Some Mexican bishops blanched when faced with relaxing control, and rebellious tradition-minded Catholics either joined ultra-right fringe groups or followed French Archbishop Marcel Lefebvre in his call for a return to preconciliar norms. Overall, however, there was a gradual move toward greater opening, stimulated from the bottom up by the SSM and the Christian Family Movement (MFC), an organization of married Catholic couples that flourished in Mexico as Catholic Action influence waned.

Already, lay Catholics had been developing a growing social consciousness as a result of seminars and retreats conducted by the Movement for a Better World and the *cursillos de cristiandad*. After Pope Paul VI invited MFC leaders José Alvarez Icaza and his wife, Luz Longoria, to be the only lay Catholic participants in the fourth session of Vatican II, the Mexican bishops named Alvarez Icaza in 1964 to be director of their new information office, called the National Center for Social Communications (CENCOS). To their chagrin, however, the bishops soon discovered that lay Catholics were not interested in mere token appointments. By 1968, after it became clear that CENCOS's mostly lay staff desired real participation and had their own ideas about the church's role in Mexican society, relations between the bishops and CENCOS began to sour.

At the same time, Father Velázquez was moving the SSM from social assistance into promotion of social activism. Hoping to refocus the church's knee-jerk anti-Communism on promotion of Catholic social action as a positive alternative, in 1964 Velázquez gathered the SSM, the MFC, the Young Catholic Workers (JOC), and more than forty other church groups into the Confederation of National Organizations (CON). The CON's emphasis on "integral development" proved an important stepping stone toward assimilation of a new pastoral methodology sweeping Latin America. Known in Spanish simply by the verbs *ver, juzgar, actuar* (literally, "to see, to judge, to act"), the method called for analysis of social reality, identification of injustices, and concerted action to overcome them. In going beyond meek criticism of inequitable distribution of wealth, the SSM and JOC were at the forefront of those denouncing ingrained social structures as the root cause of injustice. Backlash was inevitable, and when some Mexican bishops and Catholic business leaders found the analysis disturbing, the JOC was the first target and was divested by the hierarchy of its team of religious advisors.

Along with the Vatican delegate, Archbishop Luigi Raymundi, Velázquez was also instrumental in channelling efforts from a variety of church sources to help indigenous peoples. In 1959 the bishops had formed a commission on indigenous affairs, and in 1961 a semi-autonomous advisory center, called the National Center for Aid to Indigenous Missions (CENAMI), was established. Mission work among Indian communities was largely charitable until 1967, when Samuel Ruiz became president of the Bishops Commission on Indigenous Peoples (CEPI). Following Ruiz's participation in the "First Meeting on Latin American Missionary Work" in Melgar, Colombia, in 1968, the Mexican church developed a new analysis in working with indigenous people, "from the perspective of a re-evaluation of indigenous cultures."[36] Ruiz incorporated the new vision in a paper on "Evangelization Adapted to Latin America," delivered in August during the landmark Second General Conference of CELAM in Medellín, Colombia.

Both the Medellín meeting and concurrent events in Mexico made the year 1968 a watershed for the Mexican church. In February, the rise of UMAE and the increased number of dioceses were decisive in the election of Archbishop Corripio of Oaxaca as CEM president, breaking a twenty-five-year hegemony on hierarchical power held by Guadalajara's powerful Cardinal Garibi and Puebla's Archbishop Márquiz y Tóriz. In March, the CEM issued a "Pastoral Letter on the Development and Integration of the Country," which caught traditionalists off guard. Drafted by Adalberto Almeida, the fifty-two-year-old bishop of Zacatecas and then-president of the bishops' Commission on Social Work (CEPS) — aided by UMAE co-founders Ruiz and Sánchez Tinoco and an SSM team led by Father Velázquez — the pastoral letter denounced the marginalization of Mexico's poor and structural obstacles to the country's balanced development.[37] If the letter disturbed traditionalists, more disturbing was criticism of the hierarchy from priests protesting rigid ecclesiastical structures and openly calling on bishops reluctant to implement Vatican II changes to allow for greater institutional "democratization." So resistant to change were the majority of bishops that in July MFC leader and CENCOS director Alvarez Icaza publicly denounced their "absolutism" in exercising authority.[38]

As Pope Paul VI prepared to travel to Medellín to inaugurate the CELAM conference in 1968, the sharp focus of the meeting's draft document on institutionalized violence and its call for liberation of the poor from structural mechanisms of oppression was criticized continent-wide by traditionalist prelates, led in Mexico by none other than Archbishop Miranda. Many Mexican bishops saw the repressive realities outlined in the document as descriptive of South and Central America, perhaps, but not Mexico. Their assessment was proven wrong in July, when police brutality sparked an enormous student protest movement in Mexico City. By August 27, students had mobilized some four hundred thousand protesters behind a number of demands, including freedom for political prisoners and accountability for police abuse.

Pointing to Communist involvement and fearful that Mexico's image might be tarnished if protests overlapped the upcoming Olympic Games in Mexico City, the Díaz Ordaz government stepped up its use of force. On the afternoon of October 2, army troops and plainclothes police opened fire on several thousand unarmed student protesters in the Plaza of Three Cultures, also called the Plaza de Tlatelolco — in the midst of pre-Hispanic, Spanish colonial, and modern edifices symbolic of Mexico's amalgam of culture and history. At least several hundred students are now believed to have been killed. Despite attempts by the government, the military, and Mexico's pro-government media to restrict information about the massacre, the word "Tlatelolco" became synonymous with repression for an entire generation of Mexicans, and October 2, 1968, went down as a date of ignominy in modern Mexican history.

4

Medellín and the Vatican's Silent Offensive

I F THE 1968 student movement was terribly divisive for Mexican society, the Tlatelolco massacre drove a wedge between those Catholics who wanted a church of the people and those who either haltingly assimilated Vatican II reforms or wanted a return to the preconciliar order altogether. Conservative church groups had denounced the students' alleged profanation of the downtown cathedral during the huge August 27 protest. But in September laity and priests from the SSM, CENCOS, JOC, and Catholic Worker Action had joined academics from the Jesuits' Universidad Iberoamericana and Bishop Méndez Arceo in drafting a declaration "To the Mexican People," signed by thirty-seven priests and published in the press, which downplayed the supposed Communist threat and justified some of the students' demands.[1]

With Archbishop Miranda still in Medellín, the archdiocesan curia issued a statement criticizing the pro-student declaration as unrepresentative of the church's position. The day after the Tlatelolco massacre, a group of priests and religious tried to protest with a paid advertisement, which no newspaper would publish. During the following days, the Franciscans of the church of Santiago Tlatelolco, which had closed its doors to students fleeing the slaughter, refused to allow a funeral Mass to be said, and Miranda quashed attempts to celebrate memorial Masses in other Mexico City churches. Jesuit Father Enrique Maza, editor of the order's *Christus* magazine, complained that apart from Méndez Arceo, the students and those Catholics who showed solidarity with them were completely "bishop-less" during months of violent repression.[2]

A number of Mexican prelates — including Miranda, Corripio, Ruiz, and Almeida — were in Medellín at the height of the student protests, did not witness the movement's growth, and were perhaps ill-equipped to grasp its aims and ideals. Even so, there was still a marked tendency within the hierarchy to reject any movement with leftist undertones, regardless of its ideals, and to support authority against any challenge from below — be it a challenge to government or to church hierarchy. Showing a lack of sensitivity, not to mention revealing inherent sympathies toward the ruling elite, Archbishop Miranda's blessing of the official chapel for the Olympic Games on October 8 angered many who were still shocked by the massacre. The next day a CEM statement issued by Corripio mildly censured the powerful and sympathized with the government, while sharply criticizing students — both victims and survivors — for having promoted "violence, anarchic struggle, [and] disproportionate confrontation."[3]

The pro-government pronouncement fueled the polarization between most of the bishops and those Catholics hoping to advance the ideals of Vatican II and Medellín within the Mexican church. The CON's analysis in October 1968 of the "necessary change in structures for the integral development of Mexico" initiated a clash with the hierarchy that ultimately led to the group's dissolution in 1973. CENCOS separated from the hierarchy in 1969, as a result of both the Tlatelolco massacre and Alvarez Icaza's displeasure with the hierarchy's refusal to allow single mothers to join the MFC.[4] Father Pedro Velázquez died in late 1968 and was succeeded as SSM director by his brother, Father Manuel Velázquez, whose views on the need for "bottom-up" church authority contributed to the hierarchy's removal of the SSM's official status in 1970.

Despite the polarization, some prelates did push forward in the spirit of Vatican II and Medellín, most notably Bishops Ruiz, Almeida, and Sánchez Tinoco. At their prompting, in August 1969 the CEM held a special "Bishops' Pastoral Reflection" meeting to discuss Medellín's application in Mexico. Assisted by laity, clergy, and religious advisors, the bishops issued conclusions to their assembly that were remarkably self-critical, even though the self-censure was couched in palatable terms. Nonetheless, most bishops returned to their dioceses to adopt their own selective readings of Medellín. Traditionalist bishops, frightened by Medellín's conclusions, were further alarmed by Mexico's "First National Congress of Theology" in 1969, which sowed the seeds in Mexico of what would later come to be known as liberation theology. Then, following the untimely death in 1970 of UMAE promotor Bishop Sánchez Tinoco, more progressive bishops hoping to implement Vatican II and Medellín ideals in Mexico were left largely to their own devices. The UMAE experiment subsequently withered away with the disappearance in 1971 of its short-lived official successor, the Bishops Commission on Joint Pastoral Work.

While the number of dioceses and bishops grew during the 1970s, most bishops' resistance to anything more than liturgical or administrative change led to a depletion of the institutional ranks: nearly six thousand men and women religious left their orders from 1970 to 1978, and as many as twelve

hundred priests abandoned their ministry.[5] By 1979 some sixty Mexican Jesuits had left their order, dissatisfied with hierarchical intransigence,[6] while
flare-ups occurred between dissident priests and authoritarian prelates in several dioceses. The independent "Priests for the People" movement, spawned
in 1969 with publication of the bulletin Liberación, was formally constituted
in 1972, its nationwide conferences becoming a serious annoyance for a
hierarchy concerned with maintaining order.

With progressive lay Catholics increasingly alienated from their hierarchy, the bishops cut all ties to the SSM in 1973, substituting it with the
CEPS, which by virtue of having a bishop as president was more easily
controlled. Frustrated, many young Catholics opted for non-church political
activism. Some, inspired by the examples of Argentinean physician-turned-
revolutionary Ernesto Che Guevara and of Colombian guerrilla-priest Camilo
Torres, were convinced by the Tlatelolco massacre and the continued government repression to go underground and take up arms. In Mexico City,
students attending the Jesuits' Critical University Center (CECRUN) were
discovered to be involved in the urban guerrilla movement,[7] and in the
north, Catholic youth leaders like Ignacio Salas joined communist youth
counterparts in 1973 to form the umbrella Liga 23 de Septiembre, which
coordinated an armed urban movement from its base in Monterrey.[8]

Outspoken Clerics

Bishops firmly committed to the spirit of Vatican II and Medellín went their
own way. In Chiapas, Samuel Ruiz continued working toward adaptation of
traditional Catholic evangelization to indigenous reality. In 1972, with a shift
of the CELAM's leadership to the right in a backlash against liberation theology, Ruiz was ousted from the presidency of the CELAM's continent-wide
Department of Indigenous Missions. In 1974 he ended seven years as head
of the Mexican bishops' indigenous commission (CEPI) and was succeeded
as president of the commission by forty-nine-year-old Arturo Lona, bishop of
Tehuantepec, Oaxaca. That same year Ruiz organized Chiapas's pivotal first-
ever indigenous congress at the behest of Governor Manuel Velasco Suárez,
who had an important link to the local church via his cousin, Adolfo Suárez
Rivera. The latter had left the San Cristóbal diocese only three years earlier
when he was ordained bishop of Tepic by Pope Paul VI. Ruiz did not leave
the CEPI leaderless, but passed direction of the church's indigenous work
to capable and trusted successors. Under Bishops Lona, Bartolomé Carrasco,
and Jesuit José Llaguno Farías of the Tarahumara Prelature, during the 1970s
and 1980s the bishops' indigenous commission and the semi-autonomous

CENAMI advisory center elaborated "Theological Bases for Indigenous Pastoral Work in Mexico,"[9] which formalized progressive guidelines for church work among Mexico's indigenous peoples.

But perhaps no other bishop forged ahead as boldly in the spirit of both Vatican II and Medellín as did Sergio Méndez Arceo. He called for the release of political prisoners in 1969, when the government was reluctant to admit their existence. A year later, he shattered precedent by handing a letter to PRI presidential candidate Luis Echeverría calling for constitutional reforms to restore the church's legal rights — but also raising the hackles of church traditionalists by conceding that nineteenth-century reform Liberals were right in separating church and state and in divesting Catholicism of its power and wealth. In 1971 Méndez Arceo told Puebla university students that Christianity was compatible with democratic socialism, and in 1972 he was the only Latin American bishop who dared attend the international charter meeting in Chile of "Christians for Socialism," during the short tenure of the democratically elected government of socialist president Salvador Allende.

Méndez Arceo also mediated release of Guerrero state governor Rubén Figueroa, kidnapped in 1974 by the "Party of the Poor," a rural guerrilla movement operating in Morelos and Guerrero states. The previous year Monterrey business magnate Eugenio Garza Sada had been accidentally killed by the Liga 23 commandos in a bungled kidnapping attempt. Such events showed that during the decade after Tlatelolco, the tumultuous and repressive realities described by Medellín and previously deemed irrelevant by the Mexican hierarchy were, like it or not, intrinsic to Mexico itself. In some cases, the upheaval affected the church directly. A spate of kidnappings, torture, and attacks against activist priests and lay Catholics occurred throughout the 1970s, with bishops even becoming targets at times. Incidents like the violent detention in Veracruz of four Catholic bishops by heavily armed police in 1974 and the attack by gunmen on a car in which Bishop Lona was traveling in 1978 had not occurred in Mexico since the Cristero years of the 1920s.

Beginning with Bishop Almeida of Chihuahua in 1972, some Mexican prelates began identifying "institutionalized violence" as the origin of the cycle of violence and repression rocking Mexico. Almeida's position, which still shunned armed insurrection as a valid response, was supported by Bishop Manuel Talamás of Ciudad Juárez and by the Jesuits in Chihuahua's Tarahumara region. In the south, Bartolomé Carrasco, the fifty-six-year-old bishop of Tapachula, along with Samuel Ruiz and Arturo Lona, denounced the systemic violence and repression in their dioceses.[10] Inequitable land tenure seemed at the core of the problem to Hermosillo's Archbishop Carlos Quintero Arce in the northern state of Sonora, as well as to Bishop Serafín Vázquez in Huejutla, who said that repression and abuse of landless Indians fueled violence in central Hidalgo state.[11]

In 1977, when Almeida condemned the murder of an activist Chihuahua diocesan priest, Father Rodolfo Aguilar, clergy from throughout the northern states of Chihuahua, Coahuila, and Nuevo León were quick to point out that Aguilar had been martyred because of his Christian commitment to the poor.[12] In Coahuila, a dozen priests and many lay Catholics in Torreón had a history of close association with leftist grassroots organizers of land takeovers by rural and urban poor. In 1972, when a Torreón diocesan priest, Father José Batarse, became the center of a land takeover controversy that threatened to ignite poor neighborhoods throughout northern Mexico in solidarity, Bishop Samuel Ruiz was called in to mediate a peaceful settlement, which he did successfully.[13] In fact, it was the friendship between Ruiz and Bishop Fernando Romo of Torreón that provided the first link in what proved to be the unsuccessful transplant of the organizing methods used by the "Torreones" to the Lacandón jungle in Chiapas.[14]

In 1977, the seeds sown by the UMAE gave Mexican Catholicism the important administrative legacy of a reordering of the church into fourteen pastoral zones. The move served to continue dispersion of power within the hierarchy and fostered the issuance of joint pastoral letters, which carried greater weight in the denunciation of social injustice. In 1977, with Arturo Lona in his second term as CEPI president, nine bishops from Oaxaca and Chiapas inaugurated a decade of joint pastoral statements with a path-breaking letter entitled "Our Christian Commitment to the Indigenous Peoples and Campesinos of the Southern Pacific Region."[15] Individual bishops now enjoying the support of colleagues in dioceses with similar problems were also emboldened to speak out forcefully. Bishop Lona repeatedly denounced violence in Tehuantepec against campesino and indigenous supporters of a local political coalition, known as COCEI. After a 1981 COCEI-PCM election triumph in Juchitán, Lona reacted to increased repression by following Méndez Arceo's precedent in Morelos and excommunicating torturers in his diocese.[16]

Post-Medellín analysis also led some Catholic social activists and bishops to identify Mexico's fraud-ridden electoral system as a structural mechanism of oppression. Although never having campaigned for any elective office, PRI presidential candidate Echeverría — the man who as Secretary of the Interior was in charge of state security during the Tlatelolco massacre — was awarded 79.8 percent of the vote in 1970. A populist who allowed leftist political activism as an escape valve for political dissidence — while cracking down mercilessly on urban and rural guerrilla movements — Echeverría promised a "democratic opening" and did implement some political reforms. A few media restraints were eased, political prisoners were freed, and labor, political, and student organizations that accepted government subsidies or were otherwise co-opted were tolerated. But the government's total electoral control was again too apparent in 1976, when the PAN fielded no presidential candidate and another PRI politician who had never held elective office, Treasury Secretary José López Portillo, was awarded 93.48 percent of the vote.

López Portillo announced his own "political reform" in 1977, just as many bishops — after reflection upon the hierarchy's moderate document on "Christian Commitment in the Face of Social Options and Politics" (1973) — were seeing the need for a stronger church voice on the question of democracy. Prior to 1979 mid-term elections, bishops of the Gulf Pastoral Region — guided by the newly named forty-eight-year-old Archbishop Sergio Obeso Rivera of Xalapa — began the pro-democracy drive by declaring that "the totalitarian use of power [was] a form of idolatry."[17] Northern bishops were perhaps most critical in the ensuing decade of pastoral letters on politics and democracy, denouncing voter coercion in favor of PRI through "threats, layoffs, salary cuts, and handouts"[18] and condemning electoral fraud as "the foundation of the corruption that affects the country."[19]

Furor over the pronouncements on politics in violation of the constitution was fueled in 1977 by the PCM's declaration that political rights should be extended to the clergy. Shortly thereafter, in 1978, Méndez Arceo issued a joint declaration in Havana, with Nicaraguan Father Ernesto Cardenal and Spanish Communist Alfonso Comín, that a strategic alliance was needed between Christians and socialists. The CEM immediately responded that Marxism is "incompatible with Christian faith,"[20] in a statement signed by CEM president Corripio and, among others, Bishop Adolfo Suárez Rivera of Tepic, in Nayarit state. As the PCM underwent a Eurocommunist-style evolution, which led to its fusion in 1982 with other groups into the Mexican Unified Socialist Party (PSUM), the party's courtship of Catholic voters contributed to government politicians' fears of a broad church-opposition alliance against the PRI.

Indeed, many church opponents saw the hierarchy's criticism of vote fraud as an attempt to further the church's agenda through the manipulation of electoral politics, particularly in the north, where middle-class voters — disgusted by official corruption during Mexico's oil boom in 1976–82, outgoing President López Portillo's massive devaluations of the peso in 1981–82, and the nationalization of private banks — flocked to the opposition PAN. On controversial issues such as birth control, church participation in education, and amendment of the constitutional proscription on legal recognition of the church, the positions of the PAN and the hierarchy were virtually identical.

In the PAN bastion of Chihuahua, Bishops Almeida, Talamás, and Llaguno were often accused in the press of being PANistas when denouncing electoral fraud. But from the south, Bishop Lona clearly identified the campaign against the so-called political clergy as an attempt to hide Mexico's lack of democratic and human rights: "When the [northern] bishops speak out and try to raise consciousness among their people, they are accused of speaking out in favor of one party, the PAN....Here in the south, when we bishops speak of the same things around election time, we are accused of supporting the PSUM."[21]

Post-Medellín Backlash

On the church's internal front, outspoken bishops, priests, religious, and laity faced another threat, with a conservative CELAM and the Vatican backing efforts of more traditionalist Mexican prelates to re-establish authority. Méndez Arceo's open endorsement of socialism had shocked many, but at least as worrisome were expressions of autonomy at the base of the church. An embryonic Catholic feminism had met with the bishops' rejection of a draft document in preparation for the General Synod of Bishops in 1971, in which "the *virilist* or *masculinist* mentality of many bishops and priests" was denounced and the charge aired that within the church women were "more marginalized than within any other society."[22] With the pronounced religiosity of Mexican women a major sustenance of the church and the some twenty-seven thousand Mexican women religious outnumbering their male counterparts by nearly four to one,[23] the hierarchy could ill afford to promote the growth of "the suspicion of manipulation by the powers that be."[24] Méndez Arceo's reference during the International Women's Year Conference (1975) to "the significance of women in the liberation of the world and within the church of Jesus Christ" and his subsequent rejection of "simplistic condemnatory positions"[25] on abortion only served to fuel the rejection of feminism by his traditionalist colleagues.

Earning particular scrutiny from the hierarchical leadership was the growing movement of Basic Christian Communities (CEBs), which in Mexico originated virtually simultaneously in the mid-1960s in Cuernavaca and within small Bible study and Catholic social action groups in poor rural and urban areas of Guanajuato state.[26] After 1968, the CEBs began increasingly to reflect upon scripture as a means of articulating a Christian response to oppressive social structures. The movement assumed national significance after a 1972 conference in San Bartolo, Guanajuato. With the CEBs representing a means of reinvigorating the church's stultified parish structure, by the end of the decade they were receiving various degrees of support from a dozen or more bishops, most notably Bishop Rogelio Sánchez of Colima, who was an early promoter of CEBs, and prelates as generally divergent in their views as Méndez Arceo and Cardinal José Salazar López of Guadalajara. Still, the vast majority of bishops remained wary of the CEBs, as much because of the movement's lay character and semi-independence from episcopal control as its association with the precepts of liberation theology.

In fact, the anti-liberation theology backlash within CELAM also turned the tide against post-Medellín progressives in Mexico. In 1972, Cardinal Miranda began a campaign of denigration against Méndez Arceo for being out of step with fellow prelates. The campaign was taken up and repeatedly hammered home in the late-1970s by Genaro Alamilla, the diminutive and witty bishop of Papantla who occupied the important position of CEM general secretary. Adding to Méndez Arceo's estrangement from fellow bishops was his criticism of the construction of the costly new Basilica of Our Lady of Guadalupe by a coalition of church, government, and the private sector: he feared the Virgin's original liberating message was being twisted to legitimize "existing unjust and egotistical structural inequalities" in Mexico.[27]

In 1976, when Méndez Arceo, Samuel Ruiz, and Bishop José Pablo Rovalo of Zacatecas were arrested by army troops along with other Latin American bishops and clergy during a pastoral congress in Riobamba, Ecuador, the CEM was slow to express solidarity. Individual Mexican bishops criticized their colleagues' participation in the conference, and the Ecuadoran military's "national security" rationale for the arrests was virtually sanctioned later in a report written by Mexican Father Javier Lozano Barragán, then a theology professor at CELAM's Theological-Pastoral Institute and reportedly a close collaborator of the conservative CELAM general secretary, Colombian Archbishop Alfonso López Trujillo.[28]

In 1978, as CELAM was preparing for its third general assembly in the Mexican city of Puebla, Cardinal Salazar, a supporter of Vatican II reforms and of the CEBs, lashed out in a speech against "Christians for Socialism" as being an instrument of what he termed the "serious threat" to church unity and papal authority posed by ideologization of church teachings.[29] Salazar's remarks set the tone for CELAM's Puebla meeting in January 1979, when after the back-to-back deaths of Popes Paul VI and John Paul I the newly chosen John Paul II made his debut in Mexico as the "traveling pope." The object of enormous public interest, fueled partly by President López Portillo's surprise greeting of the pope on the airport tarmac as he arrived in Mexico City, the pontiff virtually stole the show from the Latin American bishops.

During five days he was greeted by massive crowds; even his critics have admitted his "extraordinary capacity to connect with the multitudes" and his "extraordinary sensitivity when faced with the circumstances and conditions he observed."[30] The pope had brought with him prepared speeches, but the poverty and outpouring of religiosity he saw in Mexico moved him to rewrite several. In Oaxaca, he told assembled Mixtec and Zapotec Indians and other campesinos that he shared the late Paul VI's desire to make the church's cause "your cause, which is the cause of the humble people, that of the poor people." He spoke to the dignity of the human person and the respect that all people merit in such eloquence that he left Archbishop Bartolomé Carrasco in tears before reporters. In Monterrey, he left the business community ill at ease after telling workers that "it is not just, it is not humane, it is not Christian to continue certain clearly unjust situations" of exploitation. Not only should Christians be concerned with the problem of unemployment, he said, but workers must themselves seek "more humane conditions" and "be treated as free and responsible human beings."

But John Paul's discourse aside, during the Puebla conference itself it was all Medellín supporters could do to maintain the general direction mapped out for Latin American Catholicism at the CELAM conference eleven years earlier. Reflecting the overall makeup of the 218 Latin American bishops in attendance, only three members of the Mexican delegation could be considered firm Medellín supporters — Bishops Talamás and Llaguno from Chihuahua state and Bartolomé Carrasco, Oaxaca's archbishop since 1976. Three others were staunch traditionalists, and two more — Cardinal Salazar and Archbishop Corripio — were appointed directly by John Paul II, who named Corripio co-president of the conference. The remainder of the Mexican delegates were vaguely centrist, influenced by Vatican II but wary of Medellín and, certainly, of liberation theology.

Despite a conservative draft document, pro-Medellín prelates did manage to salvage some of the previous conference's spirit. Among them was José Llaguno, who helped to shape Puebla's concept of the church's "preferential option for the poor," and along with Bishop Talamás joined other bishops in sending letters of solidarity to the persecuted Nicaraguan and Salvadoran churches. The Puebla document also reaffirmed the "validity" of the role within the church of the CEBs,[31] while cautiously avoiding direct condemnation of liberation theology. Prominent theologians, advisors, and progressive bishops were closed out of the meeting by the CELAM directorate, to which CENCOS responded by hosting press briefings with important figures, including liberation theologian Gustavo Gutiérrez and Salvadoran Archbishop Oscar A. Romero.

While liberation theology was not directly denounced at Puebla, by 1980 Latin American church conservatives and the Vatican were managing to stem its rapid advance. In the case of Mexico, as early as 1972 the Vatican had been concerned that movements like "Priests for the People" and "Christians for Socialism" should not further undermine church-state relations.[32] In February 1978, Rome assigned Archbishop Girolamo Prigione, a fifty-six-year-old Vatican career diplomat who had been the papal nuncio in Guatemala and El Salvador from 1969 to 1974, to be the new apostolic delegate to Mexico. A tall, solemn figure in public and a shrewd behind-the-scenes maneuverer, from his arrival Prigione set about monitoring and subsequently silencing critical voices among the Mexican bishops in an apparent endeavor to move the church out of its quasi-legal limbo existence and fully toward renewed church-state relations.

There were clear precedents to the move toward church-state detente. President Echeverría had paid an unusual visit to Pope Paul VI in Rome in 1974 and followed up the meeting by throwing Mexican government support behind construction of the Basilica of the Virgin of Guadalupe. In 1975, PRI presidential candidate José López Portillo visited some forty Mexican bishops during his campaign as part of an Echeverría-devised plan to cement hierarchy-government ties.[33] In 1977, ex-president Echeverría again met with Paul VI at the United Nations, and it is believed a church-state opening was forestalled only by the deaths of Paul VI and John Paul I in 1978. In 1979, López Portillo's surprise reception of John Paul II at the Mexico City airport and former President Miguel Alemán's meeting with the pope at Prigione's residence were further indications that the Mexican state was willing to trade concessions with the Vatican — just at a time when the chorus of Mexican bishops criticizing social inequities and institutional violence had become bothersome for the government.

With the López Portillo administration discredited during its last year in office by growing charges of corruption and a growing economic crisis, both the leftist PSUM and the conservative PAN were evolving as worrisome PRI opponents for the 1982 election. Largely under the influence of Gilberto Rincón Gallardo — a former Catholic catechist, ex-PAN supporter, and PSUM central committee member — the leftist party published a campaign brochure in 1981 making clear overtures to progressive Catholic voters. Referring to Marxism as "intrinsically perverse,"[34] Mexico City's Cardinal Ernesto Corripio — who had deftly moved from being the world's youngest Catholic prelate in 1956, through the archdioceses of Oaxaca and Puebla to Mexico City, where in 1979, at age sixty, he was appointed cardinal by Pope John Paul II — roundly rejected any attempt at rapprochement with Marxists. Corripio and his auxiliary bishops, led by the newly appointed Genaro Alamilla — who from his youth retained memories of ultra-left excesses against the church during the Cristero era — issued their own brochure, declaring that "voting for a Marxist is contrary to Christian faith."[35]

The 1982 elections saw 71 percent of the presidential vote go to PRI candidate Miguel de la Madrid — the former Secretary of Planning and Budget
who had never held elective office, but as a childhood friend of López Portillo
was handpicked by the outgoing president. Discontented voters had shifted
to the PAN, which increased its share of the vote to 17.9 percent, and the
PSUM ran a distant third. During the De la Madrid administration (1982–
86), the multiplicity of voices within the Mexican hierarchy — caused by the
expansion of the number of dioceses to seventy-three — contributed to the
church's public pronouncements on a variety of issues.

Along with the traditional remonstrances over reform of constitutional
limitations on church activities, particularly in education, the bishops frequently fretted publicly over the growth of the so-called religious "sects,"
mostly Evangelical churches whose membership had doubled in the 1970s.
The fact that the Evangelicals accounted for less than 4 percent of the total population puts the Mexican hierarchy's near-obsession with their growth
in proper perspective. In less traditional church areas such as immigration, northern bishops like Emilio Berlie Belaunzarán of Tijuana and Carlos
Quintero Arce of Hermosillo were at the forefront of prelates in criticizing
restrictive U.S. immigration policies and setting up shelters and dispensaries
for homeless immigrants in border dioceses. At the same time, they did
not neglect to blame the Mexican government for the abandonment of the
countryside, which contributed to the migration of Mexican workers to the
United States.

The bishops' commission on refugees took greater interest in Mexico's
southern border region, backing efforts by the bishops of the Southern Pacific
region to assist Central American refugees, most of whom were Guatemalan
Indians who had crossed into Chiapas in the early 1980s to escape widespread human rights abuses by the Guatemalan military. And several bishops
entered the anti-nuclear fray in the late 1980s, with Bishops Fernando Romo
and Luis Morales Reyes of Torreón speaking out in April 1986 against a proposed nuclear plant in their diocese, and the bishops of Veracruz, again led
by Archbishop Sergio Obeso, calling in December 1988 for conversion of the
controversial Laguna Verde nuclear plant to alternative energy use.

Political Corruption and Economic Deterioration

But even as the bishops continued to criticize the government on a variety of issues, Prigione worked behind the scenes to foster dialogue between
bishops lead by CEM president Obeso and PRI government officials — the
vast majority of whom were Catholic-educated, and ironically so, given a

constitution that technically banned church schools![36] Faced with the retirement and deaths of old-guard bishops born before the Cristero era, Prigione
was at the same time in a key position to advise the Vatican on replace-
ments. From 1978 to 1988, he was instrumental in the selection of thirty-one
new bishops — more than 30 percent of the entire hierarchy. One-third of
the new appointments were among the outspoken bishops of the Southern
Pacific, North, Northwest, and Gulf pastoral zones, with an additional key
appointment to the diocese of Tehuacán, where a regional seminary using
the post-Medellín technique of "insertion" among the poor had been training
priests for the entire Southern Pacific region.

When seventy-five-year-old Sergio Méndez Arceo submitted his mandatory resignation in 1982, Prigione also shepherded the appointment to
Cuernavaca of Bishop Juan Jesús Posadas Ocampo of Tijuana. Posadas, fifty-
six, had shown considerable administrative and fund-raising talents during
twelve years in Tijuana, where a feather in his miter had been the construction of an elegant new seminary. In Cuernavaca, Posadas initiated the
dismemberment of Méndez Arceo's "liberationist" pastoral policies, removing
progressive clergy from decision-making posts and promoting the Catholic
charismatic movement as a counterweight to the CEBs.[37]

After the PAN's share of the vote had jumped from 6 to 16 percent in
1983 local elections, charges of electoral fraud marred nationwide mid-term
elections in July 1985. But hardly had the electoral controversy quieted down
than two disastrous earthquakes struck Mexico on September 19–20, dev-
astating large parts of the capital and Pacific coastal areas, killing twenty
thousand in Mexico City, and leaving neighborhoods destroyed and thousands homeless. Faced with a slow government response, ordinary citizens
took rescue and relief efforts into their own hands, spawning an awareness
that Mexico's *sociedad civil* could not rely on the government to resolve
their problems. Their solidarity later flowered into hundreds of neighborhood
associations and was a key factor in the nationwide mushrooming of independent non-governmental organizations (NGOs) — which had first arisen
with Guatemalan refugee relief aid in 1980 and had already begun to spread
to the area of human rights by mid-decade.

In fact, the grassroots CEBs were among the first groups to organize
earthquake relief efforts in many areas, boosting their esteem within their
communities and contributing to the movement's growth. Indeed, as the
decade wore on, the tens of thousands of members of nearly four thousand
CEBs nationwide could count on greater episcopal support, their backers
including two-term CEM president Archbishop Obeso and fourteen other
bishops from the Northern, Southern Pacific, and Western pastoral zones. At
the forefront of large-scale quake relief efforts was the institutional church,

through creation of a Catholic Assistance Fund (FAC), which channeled international aid to earthquake victims. Under the direction of Jesuit Father Enrique González Torres, the FAC set up eight aid centers in Mexico City and organized work cooperatives for those left jobless, as well as low-cost housing projects for homeless quake victims in both the capital and the Pacific coast city of Ciudad Guzmán, Jalisco.

Meanwhile, with the anti-drug campaign getting dirtier in Mexico, the bishops also began to speak out on growing human rights abuses accompanying army and federal anti-narcotics police sweeps through remote areas. In March 1984, bishops of the Southern Pacific region condemned the "complicity of top government officials" in drug trafficking and the fact that the impoverished campesinos cultivating marijuana and opium poppies for drug lords were always "the first victims of repression."[38] With the Defense Secretary, General Juan Arévalo Gardoqui, and Interior Secretary Manuel Bartlett under increased scrutiny for alleged involvement with drug traffickers — especially after the murder of U.S. Drug Enforcement Administration agent Enrique Camarena in Guadalajara in 1985 — bishops in Guerrero state privately decried military abuse of poor campesinos in anti-drug sweeps, but said they had not gone public with denunciations due to fear of reprisals.[39]

On the election front, massive vote fraud in Chihuahua state balloting in 1986 led local bishops to call a statewide boycott of Sunday Masses in protest. Archbishop Almeida later revealed that Prigione not only personally requested the PANista mayor of Chihuahua, Luis H. Alvarez, to end a protest fast over the fraud, but at Bartlett's request he also secured Vatican Secretary of State Cardinal Agostino Casaroli's direct intervention to halt the boycott on the grounds that it violated canon law.[40] By mid-1988, Prigione had implemented Vatican imposition of administrative coadjutors in the archdioceses of Chihuahua and Oaxaca and the diocese of Ciudad Juárez, limiting the power and critical voices of Bartolomé Carrasco, Adalberto Almeida, and Manuel Talamás — all of whom were in their seventies but still very lucid and a few years yet from mandatory retirement. He also saw to Posadas's reward for his performance in Tijuana and Cuernavaca with the important appointment to the Guadalajara archdiocese in 1987, placing him in line to succeed seventy-seven-year-old José Salazar López as Mexico's next cardinal. Once in Guadalajara, Posadas again showed himself a patron of the Catholic charismatic movement, supporting establishment there of the Latin America headquarters of the worldwide charismatic groups "Evangelization 2000" and "Lumen 2000."[41]

With the glutted world oil market sending Mexico's economy on a downward spiral, with constant peso devaluations and a soaring foreign debt of $98 billion, the De la Madrid administration began to come under increasing international pressure from abroad. The International Monetary Fund (IMF) was insisting Mexico adopt neoliberal austerity measures in exchange for future credits, while the U.S. government wanted Mexico to halt the activities of international drug traffickers operating from its territory. On the debt question, Mexican bishops were vocal in insisting that not only had foreign lender banks induced Mexico to borrow ever greater sums, but bishops like Carlos Talavera of Coatzacoalcos placed partial blame on past "errors committed by [Mexican] government leaders."[42]

Meanwhile, the quality of life for Mexicans of all socio-economic strata was slipping away. In Mexico City, still not recovered two years after the quakes, an estimated fifteen hundred new migrants daily had swollen the population to 18 million — representing nearly a quarter of all Mexicans. The capital's residents generated ten thousand tons of solid waste daily, some 25 percent of it dumped on streets or illegally incinerated, adding to air pollution that had increased 150 percent since the mid-1970s — most of it caused by sulfur-rich leaded gasoline sold by the untouchable government oil monopoly, PEMEX. The *sociedad civil* effervescence following the quakes helped revive Mexico's repressed student movement in the winter of 1986–87, as academic reforms introduced without student or professor consensus by Jorge Carpizo MacGregor, rector of Mexico's National Autonomous University (UNAM), sparked massive student protests. Nationwide, the government's popularity was at an all-time low, inextricably linked in the public's mind with drug trafficking, human rights abuse, and the kind of debauchery associated with the likes of General Arturo "El Negro" Durazo, the jailed former Mexico City police chief whose graft-gotten palatial homes were legendary.

Discontent over repeated electoral fraud was compounded by an intractable economic crisis that had seen Mexico's foreign debt soar to $109 billion and its currency devalued more than 2,000 percent since 1976. The bank nationalization in 1982 had stolen the life savings of many; then, in October 1987, thousands of small investors coaxed into playing the stock market were victimized when the market lost 29.9 percent of its value, in part due to insider trading and speculation. Amid such a climate, in the fall of 1987 the PRI held its traditional six-year sweepstakes among pre-presidential candidates to see who would succeed the outgoing president.

Among six hopefuls figured the most-trusted De la Madrid administration politicians, including Bartlett and Carlos Salinas de Gortari, a thirty-nine-year-old Harvard-educated economist who had succeeded De la Madrid as Secretary of Planning and Budget in 1982. The list of *los presidenciables* did not suit everyone in the party, however. A populist "democratic current" — formed in October 1986 by ex-UN Ambassador Porfirio Muñoz Ledo and Cuauhtemoc Cárdenas, son of former President Lázaro Cárdenas —

threatened to walk out over the party's apparently irretrievable shift to the neo-liberal right.

A church spokesman had told Western diplomats in Mexico City that the hierarchy's favored candidate was Interior Secretary Bartlett, a skilled political negotiator who was seen as owing Prigione a political favor over the Vatican's intervention to halt the Chihuahua liturgical boycott.[43] But it was the new group of young PRI technocrats — mostly foreign-educated economists fostered by De la Madrid in the Secretariat of the Treasury and the Secretariat of Planning and Budget — who won the contest. Although Salinas had also never held an elected public office, on October 4 he was unveiled as PRI presidential candidate at a gala ceremony. It was not, however, a propitious beginning. Octogenarian labor boss Fidel Velázquez showed the displeasure of the PRI-affiliated Mexican Workers Confederation (CTM) with Salinas's selection by boycotting the ceremony, and within days the Cárdenas-led "democratic current" split with the party and announced its decision to mount a challenge in the upcoming national elections of July 1988.

Mexican revolutionary Emiliano Zapata, whose name inspired the recent Zapatista uprising in Chiapas.

The execution of Jesuit Father Miguel Pro, martyr of the Cristero rebellion in 1927.

In October 1968, before the opening of the Mexico City Olympic Games, soldiers fire on student demonstrators in the Plaza de Tlatelolco. Several hundred students are believed to have died.

Prophetic bishop of Cuernevaca, Sergio Méndez Arceo.

In 1979, Pope John Paul II makes his first trip outside the Vatican to attend the opening of the third meeting of the Latin American Bishops' Conference (CELAM) in Puebla, Mexico.

The Latin American bishops at Puebla proclaim the church's "preferential option for the poor."

In 1991, Tzotzil Indian women in Chiapas carry images of the Virgin of Guadalupe as they protest the imprisonment of a local priest arrested on charges related to a land takeover by peasant farmers.

Bishop Samuel Ruiz of San Cristóbal de las Casas in Chiapas. His evangelization of the Indians has stressed social justice and cultural survival.

Cardinal Adolfo Suárez
Rivera of Monterrey.

Archbishop Girolamo Prigione, Vatican
representative to Mexico.

Cardinal Juan Jesus Posadas Ocampo,
Archbishop of Guadalajara, who was
killed in the cross-fire of an airport
shootout in 1993.

Indian couple at a military roadblock in San Cristóbal de las Casas in Chiapas, after the Zapatista uprising in January 1994.

Before peace talks with the government, Zapatista rebels in the Cathedral of San Cristóbal de las Casas in Chiapas listen to views of Mexican opposition political parties in February 1994. In the center is Subcommander Marcos.

During August 1994 elections, poll workers count ballot sheets by candle light.

Outgoing President Carlos Salinas de Gortari pauses during his last state of the union speech on November 1, 1994. He is continuously jeered and shouted down by the opposition, one of whom displays a banner: "Salinas, you lie!"

Newly elected Mexican President, Ernesto Zedillo.

Bishop Samuel Ruiz,
named as a negotiator
between the government
and the Zapatista rebels.

5

Salinismo, the Church, and Quid Pro Quo

N O SOONER HAD Carlos Salinas begun his run for the presidency than he encountered obstacles on the campaign trail. In November, student takeovers of UNAM-affiliated preparatory school classrooms and a student strike at the National Polytechnic Institute (IPN) threatened to revive mass demonstrations. Then, when peso speculation provoked a major devaluation and further capital flight, the lame-duck De la Madrid administration was forced in December to compel labor and business leaders to sign a so-called Economic Solidarity Pact (PSE). The *pacto* hiked the daily minimum wage 35 percent by February to $3.80 U.S., but austerity measures included 85 percent increases in gasoline, electricity, and long-distance telephone rates. With annual inflation running at 140 percent, CTM labor boss Fidel Velázquez threatened to pull labor's support from the pact, reflecting Salinas's unpopularity with many labor unions.

Salinas's political opponents clearly smelled blood, with conservative PAN candidate Manuel Clouthier advocating civil "resistance," while "satellite" parties, previously loyal to the PRI, backed Cuauhtemoc Cárdenas's independent presidential bid under the center-left banner of the National Democratic Front (FDN). A concerned hierarchy began to consider the implications of the political scenario for the institutional church. At least since 1986, Prigione's contacts with the De la Madrid administration had facilitated secret meetings in the Vatican delegation between Mexican bishops and top government officials.[1] But with the political opposition at the PRI's doorstep, Salinas, who as the "official candidate" was supposed to assume De la Madrid's mantle, seemed reluctant to take a clear stance on church-state relations.

In February, Salinas declined to respond to a survey by the newspaper *La Jornada* in which four of the other five candidates said they favored greater religious freedom in Mexico. Surprisingly, of those who did respond, Cárdenas was more antagonistic toward the church and even seemed further to the "left" than Heberto Castillo, candidate of the Mexican Socialist Party (PSM), and Rosario Ibarra, of the Trotskyist Revolutionary Workers Party (PRT). Advocating clear church-state separation, Cárdenas revived the old Jacobin anti-church rhetoric with an undiplomatic reference to "corporations and concentrated economic powers that tend toward the feudalization of society."

A populist in the Echeverría mold, Cárdenas, on the fiftieth anniversary of his father's expropriation of foreign oil companies in March, called for a moratorium on some $7.8 billion of annual interest payments on Mexico's foreign debt. Workers and the poor were bearing the brunt of the PSE's austerity measures — believed to have been the result of pressure from the IMF. As such, a debt moratorium had considerable support and was even favored by some within the church: Emeritus Bishop Méndez Arceo had termed Fidel Castro's call for a continent-wide moratorium a "prophetic appeal" during a debt conference in Havana in 1985. But the leadership of the Catholic bishops' conference had already given its nod to the government's approach of a non-confrontational, negotiated settlement to the debt crisis. Indeed, they even participated financially in the solution, accepting government authorization to participate as a privileged partner in debt-for-equity swaps.

The swaps were rooted in a deal engineered by Father González Torres in 1986, when the Caritas-affiliated FAC — renamed the Foundation for Assistance to the Community — used part of $8 million in quake relief funds to provide low-interest loans for quake victims toward purchase of houses built on quake-damaged properties expropriated by the government. After the U.S. Treasury approved a debt-for-equity swap program to help trim Mexico's foreign debt in December 1987, the government authorized church participation in the plan to the tune of $6 million — much before Mexican environmental and development NGOs joined in the program. With González Torres serving as church broker, foreign donors to Mexican church ventures bought discounted Mexican debt from creditor banks, then donated the paper on the debt to the FAC, which traded it back to the government for hard cash.[2] While needy people were undoubtedly helped, the close church-state financial ties led to criticism of the hierarchy — both from the CEBs and from within the Jesuit order — and somewhat sullied the reputation of González Torres, his shadowy deals prompting some detractors to dub him the "Black Priest."

Such criticisms, however, bothered the hierarchy less after six decades of church life in semi-legal limbo than did the prospects for the institutional church in the immediate future. Reflecting the bishops' concern about Salinas, Mexico City Auxiliary Bishop Genaro Alamilla, president of the bishops' social communications commission, said during a press confer-ence at the CEM's April 1988 assembly that bishops who had interviewed the presidential candidates found that Salinas did "not take seriously" the idea of church-state rapprochement. At the same press conference, Bishop Samuel Ruiz said he had spoken privately with both Cárdenas and Salinas and that the PRI candidate's church-state position amounted to "idle words."

The Dubious Victory of Carlos Salinas

No sooner had the bishops issued a pastoral letter on democracy and elec-tions, asking the government to ensure "free and truly democratic elections, respecting the votes of each party," than the presidential race took an unex-pected turn in late May. Following a massive Cárdenas rally at the UNAM campus, a voter opinion poll showed the percentage of the Mexico City elec-torate favoring Salinas had slipped to 45 percent. Cárdenas, meanwhile, had surprisingly moved into second place with 26 percent — a fourfold increase in his support since December. Then, with just a month to go before the July 6 vote, PSM standard-bearer Castillo withdrew from the race in favor of Cárdenas, calling for the opposition to unite behind the center-left FDN candidate. As support for Cárdenas snowballed in the campaign's final weeks, Mexican bishops issued individual appeals to voters to overcome apathy and called for rejection of vote fraud. Interestingly enough, two key Prigione ap-pointees — Archbishop Posadas of Guadalajara and Bishop Luis Reynoso of Cuernavaca — emphasized that Catholics were obliged to cast ballots only for those candidates representing the best opportunity for increased religious freedom. Cárdenas clearly did not fit the category.

The crisis that rocked the PRI government on election day sent Salinas scrambling for support from any quarter — including Mexico's Catholic bish-ops. Amid reports of widespread irregularities, the computer system of the Federal Electoral Commission (CFE) mysteriously "crashed" on election night after early returns showed Cárdenas in the lead. That same night, the PAN's Clouthier joined Cárdenas and PRT candidate Ibarra in alleging massive vote fraud, and within hours Cárdenas disputed the PRI's claim to victory with his own figures, showing him in the lead with 38.8 percent of the vote. To most observers at the time, it seemed possible that the PRI had lost its first presidential election in nearly sixty years.

Fiction could not be stranger than what occurred next, however. After a week of restricted access to computer returns and with just 55 percent of polling stations reported, the CFE declared Salinas the winner on July 13 with 50.36 percent of the total vote. Cárdenas was declared runner-up, with 31.2 percent of the vote. Within three days, the opposition candidate drew more than three hundred thousand angry demonstrators to the downtown Zócalo main square, kicking off a nationwide protest campaign that lasted through December. But even massive protests did not stop the PRI from claiming a congressional majority, which then rubber-stamped Salinas's victory and paved the way for his inauguration on December 1, 1988.

With the exception of a pastoral letter from Bishop Reynoso — which insisted that protest be peaceful and directed to the "corresponding authorities,"[3] in this case Bartlett and the PRI-dominated CFE — the bishops' conference as a whole was silent for a full seven weeks of turmoil following the elections. Finally, on August 26, the nineteen-member CEM Permanent Council — nine of whose members where either Prigione-era appointees or markedly conservative — issued a cautious pastoral letter, admitting that "systematic disinformation and irregularities" had occurred during the electoral process, but calling on Catholics to reject violence and "to opt for civic and political participation within legal channels."[4]

What Mexican Catholics did not know at the time was that even in the midst of electoral turmoil their bishops had continued to meet secretly in the Mexico City residence of Archbishop Prigione with "civil authorities," later identified by CEM president Archbishop Obeso only as "persons of special significance in the life of the country."[5] The precise identity of those authorities is still a mystery to most. But it can be surmised that they included Bartlett, who as Interior Secretary not only engineered the election results, but was directly in charge of church affairs and had previously negotiated with Archbishop Prigione the quashing of the threatened Mass boycott in 1986 in Chihuahua.

In September, on the heels of the ratification of Salinas's victory by the PRI majority in Congress, the vacationing Vatican delegate, Prigione, joined a group of Mexican bishops traveling to the Vatican on their mandatory quinquennial *ad limina* visits. Normally, Mexico's bishops make their *ad limina* visits in three groups roughly corresponding to the northern, central, and southern regions of the country. This time, however, the Mexican bishops were to be present at John Paul's beatification of Juan Diego, the sixteenth-century Indian who was blessed with the Virgin of Guadalupe's apparition. Even so, the beatification ceremony itself hardly explains the extraordinarily high level of the Mexican church delegation: among the thirty-seven prelates were seven of Mexico's twelve archbishops; five of six members of the CEM presidency; sixteen of nineteen CEM Permanent Commission members, including the representatives of all fourteen pastoral regions; and nine of the CEM's eighteen standing commission presidents.[6]

What counsel each and every bishop received during his individual meeting with the pope has never been revealed. But what is certain is that the bishops returned to Mexico and continued their close dealings with PRI government officials. On October 25, they received authorization to increase their participation in the debt-for-equity swap program by another $15 million.[7] Then, during a mid-November CEM assembly, Archbishop Obeso told fellow prelates that the Prigione-sponsored meetings with government officials had reaped "tangible results [that] are beginning to appear on the horizon.... It seems the day is not far when a de facto situation, which unfortunately is usually qualified with the term 'tolerance,' will become [a situation] of law."[8] When compared with the bishops' remarks about Salinas in April, Obeso's comments indicate clearly that sometime between April and November — precisely during the months of electoral unrest — the bishops had been given to understand by PRI government officials that they could expect legal recognition of the church under a Salinas administration.

It is hardly any wonder, then, that faced with a choice of either Salinas or Cárdenas — the latter perhaps the true president-elect, but known for his anti-church sentiments and unable to assume power except through violent protest — the CEM leadership chose to support Salinas. But even with the hierarchy leadership in full support of the president-elect, the ninety-one bishops attending the CEM assembly in November were unable to reach a consensus for a joint declaration on the elections. Ultimately, the nineteen-member Permanent Commission's tepid pastoral letter of August was left to stand as the bishops' official word on the democratic debacle of 1988.

Hierarchical consensus was also tested over a choice of Obeso's successor as CEM president. During the assembly the balloting went to three rounds, with moderates and progressives rejecting the conservative Prigione ally, archbishop of Guadalajara and virtual cardinal-elect Posadas, and traditionalists and Prigione loyalists blocking the election of the more moderate Archbishop Manuel Pérez-Gil of Tlalnepantla. The compromise choice was Archbishop Adolfo Suárez Rivera, the sixty-one-year-old former San Cristóbal diocesan priest and UMAE team member, who had presided over the Tepic diocese before being chosen in 1984 to head the important northern archdiocese of Monterrey. Suárez's tendency to avoid conflict and seek compromise assured unity among the bishops, but it also contributed to a power vacuum at the apex of the Mexican hierarchy at a time when assertive leadership was needed.

Ready to assume the leadership role was Archbishop Prigione, who on December 1 led a delegation comprised of Archbishops Suárez Rivera, Posadas, and Pérez-Gil, Cardinal Corripio and the abbot of the Basilica of Guadalupe, Father Guillermo Schulemberg Prado, to Salinas's inauguration — the first time Catholic prelates had attended a presidential inauguration since the revolution. The CEM leadership's presence symbolically bestowed the hierarchy's "blessing" on the new president, who in turn showed himself intent upon returning the favor, proclaiming in his inaugural address that his government would proceed to "modernize" church-state relations.

Human Rights Issues

Once Salinas was installed as Mexico's de facto chief of state, his overall theme of modernization and his bold moves to assert control over the country captivated public attention. Salinas appointed to the Interior Secretariat a hard-liner, Francisco Gutiérrez Barrios, a military officer on permanent leave who in 1968, as director of the Interior Secretariat's Federal Security Directorate (FDS), had played a murky role in the massacre of students at Tlatelolco. The new president also ordered the spectacular capture of major drug trafficker Miguel Angel Félix Gallardo, as well as stock brokers accused of insider trading and speculation, and he used the army to arrest PEMEX union leader Joaquín "La Quina" Galicia Hernández — charged with corruption and illegal possession of arms, but whose arrest was seen by many as punishment for his behind-the-scenes support for Cárdenas.

Meanwhile, political repression and rights abuses against Cárdenas supporters jumped sharply, especially following the move in April to replace the loose FDN coalition with a new party, baptized the Party of the Democratic Revolution (PRD). The growing number of non-governmental human rights groups denounced the increased rights violations, among them the Jesuit order's two-year-old Miguel A. Pro Juárez Human Rights Center and the Dominicans' Fray Francisco de Vitoria Human Rights Center. Founded in 1984, the Fray Vitoria center was in the vanguard of growing church participation in the human rights movement, as was the Commission in Solidarity and Defense of Human Rights (COSYDDHAC) in the northern state of Chihuahua, presided over by Jesuit Bishop Llaguno of the Tarahumara region and housed in the Chihuahua archdiocesan offices. In Chiapas, Bishop Ruiz formed the Fray Bartolomé de las Casas rights center in January 1989 after violence against independent indigenous and campesino activists escalated following the inauguration of Governor González Garrido in 1988.

The new governor of Chiapas, the grandson of Tomás Garrido Canabal, the Tabasco state politician who was the scourge of the church in the 1920s and 1930s, had *carte blanche* to deal with political dissidence by virtue of family ties to President Salinas. The link was González Garrido's father-in-law, Antonio Ortiz Mena, who also happened to be Salinas's uncle. After seventeen years as head of the Inter-American Development Bank, Ortiz Mena had resigned in 1987 and, with few in Mexico ever daring to openly criticize first-family nepotism, Salinas appointed his uncle in 1988 to the general directorship of BANAMEX, one of the largest of the Mexican banks nationalized in 1982.

Not only did rights abuses increase under cousin González Garrido in Chiapas, but the Jesuits' Pro center noted a nationwide 50 percent increase in political murders and torture and a 1,000 percent increase in other rights abuses in some parts of the country during Salinas's first year in office. While many violations were part of a backlash against PRI opponents, a report by the U.S.-based rights group Americas Watch in June 1990 blamed anti-narcotics agents of the Federal Judicial Police for a majority of the abuses. Indeed, cultivation of opium poppies was on the rise, Mexico was on the way to becoming the prime exporter of heroin to the U.S. market, and the Salinas administration had stepped up drug seizures and arrests in its attempt to please the U.S. government. The Americas Watch criticisms of rights abuses accompanying search-and-seizure efforts echoed several years of church denunciations of police and army brutality against mestizo and indigenous campesinos. Forced by poverty into cultivating opium and marijuana, the campesinos bore the brunt of the anti-drug campaign while traffickers who supplied drug seeds almost invariably escaped apprehension.

As Mexico's rights problem continued unabated, the CEM had decided in 1988 to request its social affairs commission, the CEPS, to develop a project for a network of diocesan human rights offices.[9] By mid-1990, the network was ready to be set up but ran into a delicate situation, following the government's embarrassment over the murder of rights activist Norma Corona in Sinaloa state and subsequent death threats against political columnist and Salinas critic Jorge G. Castañeda. As Salinas tried to stave off international criticism and regain credibility through the rapid formation of a governmental National Human Rights Commission (CNDH), the CEM project quietly ground to a halt. Backing away from the planned diocesan rights network, the hierarchy shelved the project until after the conclusion of sensitive church-state negotiations; it was revived at a national meeting of diocesan social workers in September 1992.[10]

With "modernization" of church-state relations in the balance, the majority of bishops seemed willing to accept Salinas's modernizing program in other areas. In January 1990, Archbishop Suárez Rivera and FAC director González Torres were among Mexican church leaders giving their nod to the Salinas administration's renegotiation of Mexico's foreign debt, during a summit meeting in Washington, D.C., with U.S. Catholic bishops, business leaders, and officials of the World Bank and the IMF.[11] Following that meeting, in February Salinas named ex-Supreme Court Chief Justice Agustín Téllez Cruces as his personal representative to the Vatican. Pope John Paul II reciprocated in April, with the appointment of Archbishop Prigione as his personal envoy to the Mexican president.

Church-State Cooperation

While Mexican bishops were engaged throughout 1989–91 in closed-door meetings with government officials aimed at reforming Mexico's constitution in church matters, Prigione's presence as Vatican representative gave clear impetus to the talks. As the Vatican moved to undercut liberation theology throughout Latin America in the 1980s, in Mexico Prigione implemented a policy aimed at neutralizing any bishop whose critical view of the government proved an obstacle to cordial church-state ties. Turning Vatican attention to Mexico's Southern Pacific pastoral region, in 1985 apostolic visitors assigned by the Holy See made a trip to Tehuacán in an attempt to rein in the outspoken Bishop Lona. Then Prigione oversaw appointment of a young priest from northern Durango state, Norberto Rivera, to the diocese of Tehuacán, Puebla, where the Regional Seminary of the Southeast (SERESURE) had trained more than 160 priests for the poor dioceses of Chiapas, Oaxaca, Guerrero, and Puebla states since the early 1970s.

In April 1988 Prigione cited the allegedly high incidence of violations of the vow of celibacy by priests in Oaxaca in announcing the Vatican's imposition of Héctor González, the dour forty-nine-year-old bishop of Campeche, upon Archbishop Bartolomé Carrasco as coadjutor of the Oaxaca archdiocese. González thus became the first Mexican archbishop to have been ordained to the priesthood after the inauguration of Vatican Council II in 1963. He nevertheless served much the same purpose as did Bishop Juan Sandoval Iñiguez, a forty-five-year-old priest from the Guadalajara archdiocese imposed upon Bishop Talamás as coadjutor bishop of the northern diocese of Ciudad Juárez that same month. In both cases the power of critical bishops was undercut in a move to silence them. The same method was used in January 1991, when Archbishop Almeida of Chihuahua was saddled with coadjutor archbishop José Fernández Arteaga.

Along with Bishops Lona and Ruiz, Archbishop Carrasco was a key promoter of the Southern Pacific bishops' option for the poor and the *concientización* of indigenous peoples, and many of his priests had studied at the SERESURE. With leverage over both González and Rivera in Oaxaca and Tehuacán, Prigione pushed for closure of a SERESURE training program in Etla, Oaxaca, in January 1990. Five months later, two bishops appointed under Prigione's watchful gaze, Alberto Suárez Inda of Tacámbaro and Emilio Berlie of Tijuana, traveled to Tehuacán as special Apostolic Visitors and issued a report critical of the SERESURE, which led directly to the seminary's closure in November.

Dovetailing with his Vatican mandate to restructure the Mexican church was Prigione's collaboration with Mexican Interior Secretariat officials to keep potentially "troublesome" foreign priests and religious out of Mexico. At least as early as September 1990, immigration officials working under Interior Secretary Gutiérrez Barrios were consulting the papal envoy on visa applications made by priests and religious at Mexican embassies in Latin America — and conditioning their acceptance or rejection on Prigione's recommendation.[12] It was a highly unusual situation: religious vocations aside, citizens of sovereign nations were having their Mexican visa applications reviewed by an Italian native who held a Vatican diplomatic passport and whose church technically did not exist under Mexican law! An Ecuadoran bishop, two priests, and a Brazilian nun were denied visas to attend a conference on indigenous theology hosted by CENAMI, with immigration officials telling conference organizers that another sixty participants would need a letter from Prigione before being admitted to Mexico. The practice came to light when Nicaragua's conservative Cardinal Miguel Obando y Bravo was mistakenly denied a Mexican visa he needed in order to attend a CEM assembly in November 1990. Vatican delegation and Mexican church sources said Obando's visa request was rejected when Mexican officials were unable to obtain approval from Prigione — who was out of the country at the time.

The Salinista Economic "Renaissance"

While such church-state cooperation was in full-swing, the Salinista technocrats were proceeding at a frenzied pace to modernize the mammoth state bureaucracy and the economy. The most outstanding Salinas cadres of young U.S.-educated economists from the Planning and Budget Secretariat included bespectacled Manuel Camacho, forty-three, a Princeton-educated economist and close Salinas aide, appointed mayor of Mexico City in 1988; Luis Donaldo Colosio, a charismatic thirty-eight-year-old economist and University of Pennsylvania graduate, who moved from being Salinas's presidential campaign manager to federal Senator, then PRI general secretary, and later the head of the powerful Secretariat of Social Development (SEDESOL); and thirty-seven-year-old economist Ernesto Zedillo, who had risen from an impoverished childhood to win a scholarship to Yale and who Salinas named Secretary of Planning and Budget in 1988.

The Salinas neoliberal economic policies had an immediate positive macroeconomic effect. Price and wage controls imposed under the economic *pacto* helped reduce annual inflation to double digits in 1989, ultimately cutting it to 10 percent in 1993. Central to the Salinas strategy was the wholesale privatization of state-owned companies: banks nationalized in 1982 were resold to Mexican and foreign investors, the giant TELMEX telephone monopoly was privatized, and the state divested itself of scores of enterprises ranging from mining companies to sugar mills. Within five years, 360 of the 618 companies owned by the government in 1988 had been sold off, and with the revenue the government paid down the national debt, reducing foreign debt to $96 billion by 1990 and cutting both foreign and domestic debt by some $18 billion over five years. Burdensome debt interest payments were consequently reduced from 17 percent of the gross domestic product in 1988 to just 3 percent of the GDP by 1993.

Convinced that Mexican industry needed to modernize and learn to compete with foreign producers in order to survive in a global market, the Salinistas dropped trade barriers, reformed restrictive foreign investment laws, and promoted joint partnerships between foreign and Mexican businesses. Mexican middle-class consumers were immediately thrilled over the steady stream of previously unavailable foreign goods, principally from the United States, and the Salinas policies restored private-sector confidence in the economy. The result was a reversal of the capital flight that plagued Mexico in the mid-1980s, as well as a steady increase in foreign investment.

But the Salinista economic renaissance, like the post-war "Mexican Miracle," had its problems. While reduced trade barriers led to a 30 percent growth in Mexican exports by 1990, during the same period imports jumped by nearly 45 percent — contributing to a balance of payments deficit that was not immediately offset by increased foreign investment. Liberalized trade and investment policies promised to create greater employment, but the economy was unable to provide sufficient jobs for the eight hundred thousand new workers entering the job market annually, much less for those who were chronically underemployed or had been forced to migrate to the United States during the economic slump of the 1980s. By 1991, the official unemployment rate had dropped to 3 percent, but the number of underemployed — those who work less than thirty hours a week at temporary jobs — never dropped below 20 percent of the Mexican work force during the Salinas years.[13]

The reason for the mixed performance was primarily twofold: first, by 1990 foreign investment had become increasingly speculative, destined toward the stock exchange or purchase of government bonds, rather than productive, non-*maquiladora*-oriented manufacturing. At the same time, employees of smaller Mexican businesses were being laid off at an alarming rate; an estimated sixty thousand small businesses failed in 1990 alone because their products could not compete against cheap imports. Also, small- and medium-sized businesses were closed out of co-investment opportunities by the more lucrative partnership offers being pitched to foreign investors by Mexico's business elite, dominated by a group of thirty-seven Mexican moguls who controlled the country's top seventy corporations — an estimated 22 percent of Mexico's entire GDP and some 60 percent of the shares of all Mexican companies listed on the national stock exchange.[14]

The National Solidarity Program

In large measure, official church criticism of Salinista neoliberal economic policies was stifled by the promise that the newly created National Solidarity Program (PRONASOL) would ensure economic growth with social justice. Indeed, PRONASOL seemed at first to be an innovative approach to the poverty dilemma. Claiming that global competition mandated free-market economics and federal spending cuts, Salinas argued that the Mexican government could not be expected to provide its citizens with the same level of public works and social services as it had prior to the start of Mexico's economic crisis in 1982. Nevertheless, the government pledged that it would show its "solidarity" with the estimated 41 million Mexicans living below the poverty line by matching the efforts of the private sector and local communities to prevent further impoverishment during a period of economic dislocation and readjustment.

Rhetoric aside, PRONASOL proved to be an incredible sleight of hand, with public works and social services previously provided by various cabinet-level secretariats simply shifted under the jurisdiction of PRONASOL. Using "solidarity" as its motto in a massive advertising campaign, PRONASOL's initial budget of $483 million for 1989 quadrupled to $1.7 billion by 1991. An essential part of the Salinas program to modernize Mexico, the Solidarity program strung electricity and telephone lines, repaired schools, constructed superhighways, laid sewage and water lines, and handed out property titles to poor Mexicans all across the nation.

While the centralization of public spending under Solidarity did cut back on government corruption at the local level — thereby contributing to making each *peso* spent on social programs more "efficient" — overall social spending by 1993 was actually 37 percent less than it had been in 1981.[15]

The decreased spending on social services sent Mexico sliding on the UN's Human Development Index from forty-fifth place among nations in 1991 to fifty-third place in 1993. PRONASOL could modernize infrastructure, but it did not offset lost purchasing power in the cities and the countryside caused by the Salinas policies. In 1990, 75 percent of all rural dwellers still lived below the poverty line, earning less than $437 per year, and from 1989 to 1993 wage earners nationwide saw their share of the GDP fall by $165.9 billion in real terms.[16] As the poor got poorer, the country's dollar reserves swelled from $7.3 billion to $16.7 billion between 1989 and 1993 — and the rich certainly got richer. The number of Mexicans included in Forbes magazine's list of world billionaires increased from two in 1991 to thirteen in 1993 — and nearly doubled again to twenty-three by 1994. More than half of those billionaires were direct beneficiaries of the Salinas privatization of TELMEX and the nation's banking system.[17]

In the midst of this massive concentration of wealth, some bishops did express misgivings over the "solidarity" approach to providing previously obligatory government social services. On the other hand, others were not at all adverse to accepting PRONASOL handouts, with Bishop Alamilla confirming reports that Solidarity anti-poverty funds were being used not only for social works projects but to repair churches, adjacent rectories, and parish buildings.[18] In Coatzacoalcos, Veracruz, Bishop Carlos Talavera reportedly was given $264,000 of anti-poverty Solidarity funds toward the construction of a new cathedral,[19] and Archbishop Prigione admitted to reporters that Bishop Luis Morales of Torreón accepted $165,000 of PRONASOL money to finish construction of a diocesan retreat house.[20] At the same time, the Caritas-affiliated FAC increased its participation in the debt-swap program to a total of $110 million by June 1991, in some cases matching foreign donations with PRONASOL funds in joint social assistance programs.[21]

In the midst of the PRONASOL-generated debate over wealth and poverty, Pope John Paul II paid his second pastoral visit to Mexico in May 1990 and was met with another massive outpouring of public enthusiasm. Met on the tarmac of Mexico City's international airport by Prigione, Salinas, and the Mexican president's Vatican envoy, Téllez Cruces, John Paul was whisked past huge crowds lining Mexico City streets en route to the Basilica of Our Lady of Guadalupe. There, indigenous dancers performed for the pope, while lighter-skinned middle- and upper-class Mexicans occupied the majority of pew space and mestizo masses milled outside. From the basilica, John Paul sent a mixed message regarding the role in church life offered to Mexico's eight million indigenous people: he beatified not only Juan Diego, the humble Indian who had revealed the apparition of the Virgin of Guadalupe 459 years earlier, but also the three indigenous "child martyrs" of Tlaxcala, who were killed by their own people after informing on their parents' insistence in following indigenous religious tradition — a capital offense under the Inquisition.

Following a private meeting with Salinas the morning after his basilica appearance, the pope traveled to Chalco, a sprawling shantytown an hour east of downtown Mexico City on the highway to Puebla, where he said Mass and delivered a homily before more than a million faithful. Once a lush, rural dairy farming center, Chalco had seen its population swell from twenty thousand in 1979 to more than half a million by 1990, many of its people living in makeshift housing built along mired streets lined with open sewers. In anticipation of the papal visit, Salinas himself had inaugurated the electrification of the area four months earlier and water mains were laid just a few weeks before the pope's arrival. All was paid for with PRONASOL monies, and in the weeks leading up to the visit the government spent some $700,000 in Solidarity funds just to clean up the site for the papal Mass.

In his Chalco homily, John Paul spoke of the role of the "good pastor" in defending the "weakest and most defenseless" against "false pastors," among whom the pope included those "political systems [that have] an inhuman face."[22] Two days later, the pope met with Mexican business leaders in the north-central state of Durango and told them they had a responsibility to ensure that economic growth be accompanied by social justice: "We should not forget that frequently it is the poor who are forced to make sacrifices, while those who possess great fortunes show themselves unwilling to renounce their privileges in order to benefit others."[23] John Paul seemed less prepared to address the reality of Mexico's indigenous peoples two days later in Tuxtla Gutiérrez, Chiapas. Speaking to the Indians of Chiapas with a paternalist tone, John Paul counselled them to obey the commandments, avoid vices, and not to lose hope — but offered nothing concrete as to how they might rise out of their poverty.

The pope's social message seemed to resonate within the Mexican church hierarchy. During a church-sponsored meeting of small business leaders in October 1990 church spokesman Bishop Genaro Alamilla cautioned against the increasing accumulation of wealth by both business and government. Catholic social activists like Rogelio Gómez Hermosillo, a lay advisor to the CEBs and director of Mexico City's Ecumenical Studies Center (CEE), were also pleased that John Paul spoke "so clearly and unequivocally about the reality of poverty."[24] Before the pope's arrival, lay Catholic activists and Mexican priests had written him open letters urging a papal denunciation of poverty and cautioning John Paul not to allow his visit to be manipulated for political ends by the government.[25] The possibility of manipulation of the church was echoed shortly after the papal visit, when Coadjutor Bishop Juan Sandoval Iñiguez of Ciudad Juárez raised eyebrows during a special CEM assembly, cautioning fellow prelates "not to link ourselves or even seem to be linked to a regime...lacking in democratic legitimacy in the eyes of many. The church would suffer damage if, in exchange for legal recognition, it were to be labelled an ally of the system."[26]

Although Salinas's repeated promises of forthcoming employment and "solidarity" social conscience kept most hierarchical criticism of his policies at bay, his public proposal of a free-trade agreement with the United States elicited lukewarm responses, at best, from several Mexican bishops during press conferences at their assembly in November 1990. Six months later, during their April 1991 meeting, Bishop Emeritus Genaro Alamilla again expressed the bishops' reservations and suggested the need for a national survey to determine the amount of public support for the trade pact.

The Church and NAFTA

In an attempt to overcome Catholic Church opposition to free-trade, in May 1991 U.S. trade representative Carla Hills met with seven Mexican bishops and six of their U.S. counterparts during a summit of U.S. and Mexican government, business, and church leaders in Washington, D.C. Hills's aim was to convince both U.S. and Mexican Catholic prelates of the necessity of "fast-track" negotiations, which would oblige the U.S. Congress to accept or reject without amendments a North American Free Trade Agreement (NAFTA) between Mexico, the United States, and Canada, which had since joined the free-trade talks.[27]

Returning home, Archbishops Suárez Rivera and Pérez-Gil responded to a request for a NAFTA position paper, made to them by U.S. Cardinal Daniel Pilarczyk of Cincinnati, with reservations that Mexico might be overcome by the sheer size of the U.S. economy. But they recommended the "fast-track" as the surest means of reaching the agreement, adding that NAFTA might lead to "greater democratic participation" in Mexico and increase "productivity in the countryside, modernizing the means of organization and achieving greater well-being for campesino communities."[28] Six days later, U.S. President George Bush won fast-track approval from the U.S. Congress, and on June 4, U.S. Catholic Conference general secretary, Mons. Robert N. Lynch, gave his approval to the pact, expressing the hope in a letter to Hills that NAFTA would realize its "potential benefits for the people of all three countries."[29]

That summer the government's PRONASOL campaign was put to the political test as voters went to the polls in national, state, and local elections. Since the inception of Solidarity in 1988, the government had channelled Solidarity funds to poor areas like Chalco and states like Michoacán, Guerrero, Oaxaca, Mexico, Puebla, and Veracruz — all Cárdenas strongholds in the 1988 national elections. Critics charged that the Solidarity program had political aims — and it did. Salinas himself outlined the PRONASOL ideology in a work he wrote years earlier,[30] calling for a redefinition of public spending in the countryside to regain the loyalty of campesinos to the political system. At the same time, by centralizing public spending in Salinista hands, the president created a structure for doling out largesse to voters that was parallel to the old PRI machine — and cut non-Salinista party members out of the patronage loop. In strictly electoral terms, however, the government insisted that Solidarity's benefits to PRI were indirect, with PRONASOL director Carlos Rojas repeatedly likening the program's function to public spending in any democracy where a government hopes to stay in power by giving the electorate what it wants.

As elections approached, the message of Cardenista candidates paled in the face of PRONASOL benefits delivered for more than two years by the PRI government. Battered by repression that had cost the lives of scores of PRD militants and with the party torn by political infighting, Cárdenas's fledgling PRD party also found itself isolated after its abstention from the congressional vote of 1990 that approved limited reforms to the country's electoral law. On August 18, a large voter turnout of 66 percent resulted in a rebound for PRI candidates nationwide, who won as much as 61 percent of the total vote. The two-thirds PRI majority victory in the federal Chamber of Deputies was an important milestone in Salinas's plan to fundamentally alter Mexico's economy and society, giving the party the votes necessary to amend the country's constitution.

Initially, PRD and PAN charges of fraud were echoed by the bishops' social affairs commission, CEPS, which issued a statement on August 22 criticizing the "old practices of altering ballots." But both the CEPS and Archbishop Suárez Rivera praised the large voter turnout as an important step toward "real democracy" in Mexico.[31] For the institutional church, the most important aspect of PRI's two-thirds congressional majority was that it made possible constitutional amendments proposed by Salinas during his third state of the union address on November 1, 1991. Prigione, Suárez Rivera, and seven other Mexican bishops listened attentively from their auditorium seats as Salinas gave his pledge of promoting "a new legal situation for churches" that would not threaten church-state separation, freedom of belief, or secular education in public schools.[32]

Constitutional Amendments and Underlying Unrest

On January 28, 1992, Salinas's wishes were carried out by the PRI-controlled Congress, which passed amendments to five constitutional articles, thus reversing anti-church precepts first contained in the Liberal constitution of 1857 and then broadened in the constitution of 1917: the ban on religious education was lifted in private schools; the right of religious orders to exist was recognized; open-air liturgical services were no longer prohibited; the de facto possession of private property by religious entities was legalized; and all churches and religions gained legal status and autonomy through the establishment of "religious associations." Catholic bishops were little fazed by the fact that it would take several months to pass accompanying regulatory legislation. After seventy-five years of legal limbo, they were thankful that the very existence of religion was finally recognized in Mexico's constitution.

Other amendments were not so pleasing to Catholic social activists, however, including the January 1992 reform of Article 27, which since 1917 had embodied the ideals of land and liberty for which Zapata and his followers had fought in the Mexican Revolution. The amendment was the result of the Salinas administration's belief that Mexico's campesinos would have to become agricultural entrepreneurs so that the nation could compete in the global marketplace. The reform chiefly affected the ejido communal farming system, the pillar of Mexico's post-revolutionary agrarian reform, under which the right of individuals to work the land on communally held ejido farms could not be transferred or sold to another. In February, a new agrarian law regulating the amendment broke that taboo, allowing *ejidatarios* to sell their land or to use the land as collateral for loans. An end to Mexico's revolutionary agrarian reform program was also decreed and campesinos were denied the right to file new petitions for further ejido land distribution.

Both Archbishop Bartolomé Carrasco and Bishop Samuel Ruiz were immediately critical of the amendment. In January 1992, a conference organized by Ruiz in San Cristóbal discussed the reforms and criticized the amendment as an effort by the Salinas administration to reconcentrate land in the hands of a few, resulting in monopoly agribusiness geared to competition in a free-trade environment.[33] In Tehuantepec, Bishop Lona said Mexico's indigenous campesinos, least likely to adapt to the Salinista entrepreneurial program for the countryside, would be hardest hit. With spiritual links to their ejido and ancestral lands, Mexico's fifty-two remaining indigenous groups still accounted for some 10 percent of the total population and more than a third of the entire rural population. And they were the poorest of Mexico's poor, with an estimated 65 percent living in extreme poverty and with a per capita income of less than $232 dollars per year.[34] In the spirit of Puebla's "preferential option for the poor," Bishop Lona exposed the hypocrisy of a constitutional amendment promoted by the Salinas administration to acknowledge indigenous cultural rights, while leaving some six thousand indigenous prisoners languishing in jails nationwide — many of them arrested on trumped-up charges and imprisoned without trial, often as part of ongoing attempts to steal their lands.

In 1992, Salinas hand-picked PRI General Secretary Luis Donaldo Colosio to head the new super-Secretariat of Social Development (SEDESOL), giving him jurisdiction over the Solidarity bureaucracy and spending prerogatives. But government public works programs, which were the heart and soul of PRONASOL, could not solve the fundamental problem of poverty nor quell the indigenous and campesino activism that elicited a backlash from authorities. In response to repression, Catholic human rights activists joined nearly three dozen independent Mexican human rights groups in 1991 to form the "All Rights for All" national human rights network. Rights activists like Father Miguel Concha Malo, director of the Dominicans' Fray Vitoria center, Father Jesús Maldonado of the Jesuits' Pro center, and Jesuit Bishop José Llaguno of the Chihuahua-based COSYDDHAC, were in the lead of efforts to combat apparent government indifference to the problem by focusing international attention on Mexico's poor human rights record.

In June 1992, as U.S. opponents of NAFTA began to point to Mexico's rights record as reason not to sign the trade accord, the Salinas administration elevated the governmental National Human Rights Commission to constitutional status. At the same time, with implementation of the regulatory law on religious matters virtually assured, the institutional church felt secure enough to become more involved in the human rights question. Showing a degree of independence from Prigione, Coadjutor Archbishop González of Oaxaca — president of the CEPS commission — in September 1992 chaired a meeting of Caritas and church human rights promoters in which not only was NAFTA criticized for having been negotiated "behind the backs" of the Mexican people, but the project for a national network of diocesan human rights offices was revived. Just a month later, Father González Torres set up a human rights center in the Mexico City archdiocesan FAC/Caritas office, choosing as office director well-known rights activist María Teresa Jardi — who immediately received death threats, prompting a furor in the national press.

In early 1993, Bishops Ruiz and Lona formalized their long commitment to human rights defense with registration of their diocesan rights offices as religious entities with the Interior Secretariat. But the new year held an ominous sign for non-governmental rights activists, as well as independent indigenous and campesino organizations. In the traditional cabinet shuffles prior to the choice of a new presidential successor, Salinas was expected to shift ace political negotiator Manuel Camacho from his post as mayor of Mexico City to the position of Interior Secretary in order to more effectively manage potential political and social conflict. Instead, Salinas picked his cousin, González Garrido, whose rights record as governor of Chiapas had been abysmal. To offset the public outcry, Salinas dispatched Jorge Carpizo MacGregor — who had moved from UNAM rector to Supreme Court Justice and CNDH president in just four years — to clean out the corruption-riddled attorney general's office. The appointment of Carpizo pleased some rights activists, with Jardi even accepting a job as federal district attorney in Chihuahua state, notorious for its drug trafficking and rights abuses. Still, the move of González Garrido to Interior indicated to many rights groups that Salinas intended a crackdown against them.

Death of a Cardinal

On the church front, following the deaths within weeks of each other of Bishops Llaguno and Méndez Arceo in early 1992, Archbishop Prigione began to look closely at the diocese of San Cristóbal, where Bishop Samuel Ruiz was not only heir-apparent to the leadership of progressive voices within the church, but a linchpin of the post-Medellín influence in the Southern Pacific pastoral region. A younger but more traditionalist bishop, Felipe Aguirre Franco, aged fifty-four, had been presiding over the neighboring diocese of Tuxtla Gutiérrez since 1974. A new and inexperienced prelate, Felipe Arizmendi Esquivel, fifty-two, had been appointed under Prigione's gaze in 1991 to the Tapachula diocese, vacated when Bishop Luis Miguel Cantón died in a tragic plane crash during the papal visit in May 1990.

Clearly an impediment to the Vatican efforts to redirect and control the Mexican church, Bishop Ruiz had always been careful to couch his "liberationist" reading of Christianity within the pastoral framework of his own diocese. But with the arrival in 1992 of the five hundredth anniversary of Hispanic Catholic evangelization of Latin America, his views on the need to recognize the values of indigenous culture in transmitting the faith came into conflict with those who simply wished to glorify the "spiritual conquest" of the Americas. Ruiz's calls for the church to admit "with profound sadness and almost with shame that in the entire continent in all this time there has not arisen a single autochthonous church"[35] were an embarrassment for the institutional church as the pope prepared to visit Santo Domingo for the fourth CELAM general assembly in October 1992. On the five hundredth anniversary of Christopher Columbus's arrival to the Americas, Indians in Chiapas pulled down a statue of Spanish conquistador Diego de Mazariegos in protest against five centuries of Hispanic domination. Following the CELAM assembly, Ruiz and three other Southern Pacific prelates issued a pastoral letter citing the Santo Domingo document to urge "ecclesial recognition of the original peoples of America."[36]

With the obvious goal being to undermine Ruiz's influence, Prigione certainly had an ally in former Chiapas governor González Garrido, whose membership in the Chiapas ruling elite had led to clashes with Ruiz over human and indigenous rights questions. Following the army's torture of Tzotzil villagers accused of murdering two military officers in March 1993, the powerful seemed to be lining up against the Chiapas bishop as Ruiz clashed openly with army General Miguel Angel Godínez Bravo, a powerful figure in the military and former head of the elite Presidential Guard under President López Portillo. The intervention of the Fray Bartolomé rights center in defense of Tzeltal villagers detained and tortured after a clash on May 22 between army troops and the previously unknown Zapatista guerrilla group further angered authorities. Ruiz's diocese might well have been targeted by Prigione for the imposition of a coadjutor administrator — had not a shocking occurrence intervened to forestall events.

On May 24, two days after the skirmish between Zapatistas and the army in the jungle near Ocosingo, Cardinal Posadas was killed as he arrived at Guadalajara's international airport to receive Archbishop Prigione, who was aboard a Mexican airline flight on approach to Guadalajara from Mexico City that very moment. According to an elaborate explanation by the Mexican attorney general's office, no sooner had the cardinal's automobile pulled to a halt than it was caught in a crossfire between rival drug trafficking gangs, in which Posadas Ocampo, his thirty-three-year-old driver, and five other individuals were killed.

Gunmen hired by Ramón and Benjamín Arellano Félix, cousins of jailed drug kingpin Miguel Angel Félix Gallardo and lords of a family narcotics cartel in Posadas's old diocese of Tijuana, were said to have mistakenly opened fire on the cardinal's white Grand Marquis luxury sedan, which happened to be a model frequently used by Mexican drug lords. The hit men were said to have believed that Posadas was part of the entourage of rival Sinaloa drug trafficker Joaquín "El Chapo" Guzmán, who was also arriving at the airport terminal at the same time and who managed to escape unscathed. Moments later, Arellano Félix gunmen strolled aboard a commercial flight and escaped to Tijuana. Guzmán fled the country, was apprehended in Guatemala, and was then turned over to Mexican authorities at the border on June 9, amid a wave of public outrage.

The Posadas killing caused a deterioration between the Mexican hierarchy and the Salinas government, which was exacerbated on June 24 when Archbishop González of Oaxaca and four other bishops on the CEPS commission issued a pastoral letter critical of the government and the military. Their "Pastoral Instruction on Violence and Peace" charged that "the narcotics trafficking mafia ... in particular, has bought off or has associated with a significant number of public and military officials." It was a slap in the face for the military, which since 1968 had clearly become a force for control of political dissidence and a major actor in Mexico's anti-narcotics campaign. After an immediate protest by the National Defense Secretariat (SEDENA), the CEM presidency apologized, met with top military officials, and then had the CEPS document rewritten — without the controversial reference.

With fences barely mended, another flare-up in Mexican church-state relations occurred on the occasion of Pope John Paul II's third visit to Mexico in August 1993. En route to the United States, the pope was received with all pomp and ceremony accorded a head of state during his twenty-four-hour stopover in Mérida, Yucatán. After meeting with President Salinas, he addressed Latin American indigenous leaders in Izamal and then received Mexican bishops following Mass on a 212-acre site in Mérida. It was there that Bishop Ruiz hand-delivered to the pope his pastoral letter, "In This Hour of Grace," in which he quoted Catholics in his diocese saying that "in elections, we are compelled to vote for the official party, PRI," complaining of "repression in the rural areas and in the city" as well as "generally corrupt" authorities, who placed justice "at the service of money and of the dominant political ideology."[37]

The next month, Prigione took his annual holiday in Italy. While he was away, Ruiz's reputation suffered a blow when the Mexican newsweekly *Proceso* published an article charging that Ruiz's irresponsibility had led to the growth of a guerrilla movement in the state. In October, Prigione returned to Mexico with apparent assurances from Vatican officials that Bishop Ruiz would be dealt with. On October 7, Bishop Ruiz's appointment with the Secretariat of the Interior to register the Catholic Church in San Cristóbal in accordance with Mexican law was canceled precipitously. Prigione then leaked to Mexican reporters via Bishop Javier Lozano Barragán of Zacatecas a list of the charges against Ruiz — among them, that he had offered an "interpretation of the Gospel based on Marxist analysis, providing a reductionist view of the person and work of Jesus Christ," that he had carried out pastoral work in San Cristóbal that "does not conform in all aspects to church teachings" and that excluded those who did not agree with his vision, and therefore was "incompatible with the Catholicity of the local church."[38]

Then during a press conference on October 27, Prigione himself told reporters that the charges against Ruiz had been made by the Vatican's

Congregation for Bishops, which he said was seeking Ruiz's resignation. Rec-
ognizing serious trouble, Ruiz looked for and received help from an unusual
source, his old colleague of UMAE days in the 1960s and now cardinal,
Ernesto Corripio. Prigione's relationship with Corripio had deteriorated, reportedly due to the Vatican envoy's mission since 1984 to carve up the
mammoth Mexico City archdiocese into several dioceses and wrest the Basilica of Guadalupe from archdiocesan control. Corripio provided Ruiz with one
of Mexico's top canon lawyers for his defense, Father Antonio Roqueñi, legal counselor to the Mexico City archdiocese. The bishop of San Cristóbal
proceeded to prepare his quinquennial *ad limina* report for John Paul II, and
at Christmas time issued a pastoral message in which he blamed his trouble
with the Vatican on reaction to the pastoral letter he delivered to the pope
in August. Little did he know at the time that he would shortly be the focus
of international attention as a result of the violent resurgence of Mexico's
centuries-old struggle between the powerful and the poor in the New Year's
Day rebellion by the Zapatista National Liberation Army.

Uprising, Uncertainty, Assassination

PRESIDENT CARLOS SALINAS was not to be easily located in the early morning hours of January 1, 1994. Celebrating New Year's Eve in a secluded and exclusive villa in a Pacific coastal resort, Salinas was reveling with his family in the first moments of Mexico's January 1 entry into the North American Free Trade Agreement (NAFTA). Accompanying them was another family, that of Luis Donaldo Colosio, the former SEDESOL cabinet secretary and the man who Salinas had chosen over Mexico City mayor Manuel Camacho to be the PRI's 1994 presidential candidate. Married to the daughter of former Chiapas Governor Velasco Suárez, Guadalupe, Camacho had been widowed in the middle of the Salinas term and then unknowingly "frozen" politically in the mayor's seat as Colosio was being groomed to succeed Salinas. Colosio — charismatic, handsome, and a reputed lady's man in the John F. Kennedy mold — had the technocratic credentials of the Salinas inner circle. But the forty-three-year-old PRI candidate was much more than that.

The first PRI standard bearer in thirty years to have held elective office prior to his presidential bid, as party general secretary Colosio had learned to combine strong-arm tactics and political patronage to placate the party old guard, known as the *dinosaurios,* upset over the 1988 electoral humiliation, which they blamed on the politically inexperienced Salinista technocrats. Then, as head of SEDESOL, Colosio greased the squeaky wheels of Mexico's social order with public works and social service programs in poor communities the length and breadth of Mexico.

A practicing Catholic, Colosio was raised just sixty miles south of Nogales, Arizona, in the town of Magdalena de Kino — named after seventeenth-century Jesuit missionary Padre Kino. That fact was not lost on Catholic bishops, who were generally pleased with Colosio's nomination, both because they thought he might further reform regulatory laws dealing with the church, and because they believed his Solidarity experience would put him "more in touch with the needs of the people"[1] than Salinas or the other technocrats. Some believed Colosio's background, "from a middle class, hard-working family with strong traditional Mexican family values,"[2] would promote Christian moral ethics in government and business. Although they knew, neither prelates nor press ever acknowledged that Colosio was twice-divorced — indeed, he and his third wife, Diana Laura, along with their two small children, were most often portrayed as a model family for modern Mexico.

As the first hour of the New Year drew to a close, an urgent phone call to Carlos Salinas from General Godínez Bravo in Chiapas left the president ashen-faced. He turned to Colosio and family members, dampening their New Year's NAFTA merrymaking with news that armed rebels in Chiapas had called for his own resignation and declared war on the army. As the Mexican press repeated ad infinitum, it seemed that on the night of December 31, Mexico had dreamed of entry via NAFTA into the First World, yet had awoken in the midst of a nightmare on January 1 to find guerrilla warfare confirming it was still part of the Third World. Breaking up the party, Salinas returned to the capital immediately, hoping to nip the rebellion in the bud before it damaged Mexico's international image and future economic plans. By January 6, with fighting raging in Chiapas and car bombs exploding in Mexico City, Salinas, fearing for the safety of his family, reportedly sent his wife and children out of the country and prepared to face the worse.

On New Year's Day in San Cristóbal, well-disciplined but poorly armed indigenous rebel troops passed out copies of the Zapatistas "Lacandón Jungle Declaration" as their enigmatic mestizo leader, "Marcos," conversed with tourists and journalists, his identity concealed beneath a black ski mask. The rebels' manifesto declared their rebellion a "just" war, the "product of five hundred years of struggle" against a series of conquerors, invaders, and dictators, whose aim had been to "plunder the riches of our land without caring that we were dying of hunger and incurable diseases, without caring that we have nothing — absolutely nothing — neither decent shelter, nor land, nor work, nor health, nor food, nor education, nor the right to freely and democratically elect our authorities, nor independence from foreigners, neither peace nor justice for ourselves and our children."[3]

Devoid of much of the leftist rhetorical baggage usually accompanying Latin American guerrilla movements, the Zapatistas carefully supported their demands with nationalist, patriotic, and democratic ideology. Referring to the "inalienable right" granted citizens by the constitution to alter Mexico's form of government if so desired, the manifesto called Mexico's PRI regime "a dictatorship of more than seventy years headed by a band of traitors." Calling the military the "fundamental pillar of the dictatorship," the declaration said Salinas's own presidency was "illegitimate" and urged Congress and the Supreme Court to "depose the dictator." Stressing the social needs of the indigenous population, the rebels said they would not "stop fighting until these basic demands of our people have been met, establishing in our country a free and democratic government."[4]

The nebulous concept of democracy meant but one concrete thing for indigenous Zapatistas: an end to years of manipulation by non-indigenous politicians. But the Zapatista appeal to democracy — particularly Marcos's condemnation of Salinas's personal choice of Colosio as "a clear sign that this country is heading directly toward (a second) Porfiriato"[5] — also resounded nationwide among those still resentful over the 1988 vote fraud and Salinas's unkept promises for authentic democratic reform. Cleverly designed for national consumption were appeals to Mexican nationalism and patriotism — concepts with little positive meaning for Mexico's nine million remaining indigenous people, whose major struggle since 1821 had been to survive the cultural and racial onslaught accompanying Mexican nationhood. Indeed, since 1917, that very struggle had meant resistance to forced integration into the nationalist mold of post-revolutionary modern Mexico.

The Zapatista leadership's romantic revival of the heroic ideals of "land and liberty" championed by Zapata, Villa, and their followers, also struck a sympathetic nerve among the Mexican public. With anti-Yankee sentiments ever latent among most Mexicans, the virtual U.S. dictation of terms of the NAFTA accord rankled the sensibilities of many. But, as with the notions of patriotism and nationalism, NAFTA in itself meant little to the Indians of Chiapas. Clearly, the catalyst that allowed the Zapatistas to field two thousand indigenous troops on January 1 was the chronic combination of insufficient land and degrading rural poverty, leading landless indigenous youth to join the Zapatistas in droves. The rebel leadership had impressed upon them the link between poverty and NAFTA: the opening of Mexican agriculture to free trade, said Marcos, represented a potential "death certificate" for Mexico's indigenous peoples. Bound by tradition to ritual subsistence cultivation of maize and beans, they would fail any attempt to turn them into agribusiness entrepreneurs, losing their land and culture in the process.

Free-market ideas had already taken their toll on those mestizo and indigenous campesinos in Chiapas who tried their luck with the regional cash crop, coffee. After the Salinas administration eliminated guaranteed coffee prices, along with subsidies to most other crops, a 50 percent drop in world coffee prices pushed Chiapas's campesinos back into subsistence farming of maize and beans, the only crops that retained any government subsidies.[6] They hoped that continued agrarian reform would provide them enough land to meet their family's basic needs. But the Salinas administration had decided that constitutional Article 27 needed to be amended, in order to enact legal reforms to make way for NAFTA. In one fell swoop, the amendment ended agrarian reform and dashed indigenous communities' hopes of recuperating any more of the lands taken from their ancestors through the centuries.

To buffer the short-term effects of the trade opening, the government provided credits through PRONASOL and, as of October 1993, via subsidy payments under the National Program of Direct Rural Aid (PROCAMPO).[7] But NAFTA dictated subsidy elimination by the year 2008, ultimately placing mestizo and indigenous campesinos in direct competition with mammoth U.S. agribusiness companies. The choice looked grim: Mexico's campesinos faced poverty in the long run, as maize and bean prices were to fall in the face of cheap imports from the United States and Canada; or they could escape rural poverty by cutting their ties to the land and emigrating to urban shantytowns, where they would surely lose their culture as they joined the already swollen ranks of factory laborers.

A third choice, one offered to them by the Zapatista leadership, was to take up arms and fight in an effort to try and halt the process. Thousands did exactly that, and many died in the fierce fighting following the January 1 uprising. The Zapatistas' calls for Generals Godínez Bravo and Gastón Menchaca Arias to surrender the 31st military zone base at Rancho Nuevo fell on deaf ears. Armed with old rifles and shotguns, pistols, machetes, and the occasional high-powered R-15 and AK-47 automatic weapons, early on January 2 the Zapatista contingent in San Cristóbal began a retreat that included an attack on the Rancho Nuevo base, lasting ten hours and resulting in at least twenty-four Zapatista casualties. As a result of the Rancho Nuevo assault, the military reportedly received direct orders from their commander-in-chief, President Salinas, to crush the revolt.

Sympathy for the Zapatistas

To forestall a full-scale military counterattack, the Zapatistas turned to harassment, attacking the Rancho Nuevo garrison repeatedly over the next several days. As rebels prepared their retreat into the canyons and the Lacandón jungle, a Zapatista column near Comitán took prisoner former Chiapas governor and retired General Absalón Castellanos Domínguez, a member of the local elite. Other rebel columns occupied more towns, leaving burnt public buildings in their wake as they moved toward the jungle. Altamirano was spared any major battle, but fighting continued for days near San Cristóbal, where army helicopters launched rockets and strafed retreating guerrilla columns.

In Ocosingo, Zapatistas had re-entered the town before dawn on January 1 and attacked the town hall, killing four police before the victims' colleagues surrendered. The next day, after Dominican Father Pablo Iribarren had ventured into the uneasy truce to collect the bodies and say a funeral Mass for the dead, three army battalions broke through rebel defenses, entered Ocosingo, and encountered a Zapatista rear guard of poorly armed militia in the town marketplace. The ensuing battle was fierce and included helicopter strafing of rebels in the market and of the rooftops of the San Jacinto church and Dominican rectory.[8] After three days of fighting, as many as thirty-five Zapatistas and an unknown number of civilians were dead, with shocking television images showing young men in makeshift Zapatista uniforms lying face down in the Ocosingo market — their hands tied behind their backs and dried blood on the pavement from virtually identical bullet wounds to their heads.[9]

Local and national power groups immediately blamed Bishop Ruiz's diocesan pastoral team for the rebellion. On January 1, Mexico's powerful Televisa network broadcast a rumor that the Fray Bartolomé center's director, Father Pablo Romo, was a Zapatista field commander; the thirty-two-year-old Mexican Dominican was actually in Mexico City, where he had been for the holidays. That night the Chiapas state government falsely claimed that "liberation theology Catholic priests and their deacons" in Ocosingo had allowed rebels to broadcast communiqués via a "San Cristóbal diocesan radio-communications system"[10] — which in fact did not exist. The military repeatedly entered the San Jacinto church and rectory, saying Zapatistas and arms caches were hidden there, and in Altamirano the army accused the Sisters of Charity of St. Vincent de Paul of harboring rebel sympathies.

Diocesan and Dominican spokespersons repeatedly denounced the uprising as "madness,"[11] however, saying ultimately it could only cause more harm than good for indigenous peoples. The government tried to play off Bishops Felipe Arizmendi of Tapachula and Felipe Aguirre Franco of Tuxtla Gutiérrez against Bishop Ruiz, getting them to sign a statement separately on January 1.[12] But within hours all three bishops agreed to issue a joint statement calling for dialogue and condemning the Zapatistas' recourse to violence.[13] In the face of a clear indigenous majority among the rebels, the government charges that the rebellion was "not an indigenous uprising"[14] and that the Indians had been "pressured" and "manipulated"[15] to join the movement by "a professional leadership, expert in conducting acts of violence and terrorism,"[16] seemed ludicrous. Bishop Ruiz avoided immediate comment — until Bishops Arizmendi and Aguirre Franco seemed to publicly support the charges.[17] Ruiz then responded, saying he did not believe the Zapatista rank and file were "strictly speaking, people who have been obliged or fooled"[18] into joining the movement.

While fighting raged, and Mexico's stock market plummeted, some Salinas administration officials contacted church leaders, looking for a solution to the conflict. Bishop Ruiz was asked to mediate by SEDESOL Secretary Carlos Rojas and by Manuel Camacho[19] — by then Secretary of Foreign Relations, a post he had brokered six weeks earlier after being passed over as the PRI's presidential choice. The CEM came out publicly against a violent government response,[20] and on January 4 Archbishop Prigione said Salinas had asked him personally to see to church mediation of the conflict.[21] A weekend meeting between Salinas and Mexico's ambassador to the Vatican, Enrique Olivares, along with Prigione's apparent desire to intercede, angered Cardinal Corripio, who flatly turned down a Salinas request to denounce the Zapatistas.[22] On January 6, Salinas took to the airwaves to offer a unilateral cease-fire, but insisted that the Zapatistas were "professionals of violence," a charge echoed the next day by Undersecretary of the Interior Socorro Díaz, who said the rebels were supported by "ideologues and religious of different orders."[23] Upset by the charges, Corripio and his archdiocesan team put the wheels of support for Samuel Ruiz in motion.

On January 8, as the national nerve was shaken by news of a car bomb in Mexico City and explosions in four states, Corripio dismissed the charges against the church in Chiapas as defamation and unfounded. That same day, he dispatched a delegation to San Cristóbal, which included human rights lawyer María Teresa Jardi, who was then reincorporated into the archdiocesan team by Father González Torres after resigning her federal prosecutor post to work on the Chiapas crisis. Led by González Torres, the team conferred with Ruiz over Salinas's request that Corripio denounce the rebels. The very next day, Ruiz flew to Mexico City, where on January 10 he met with Corripio and then secured support from a key church player and old friend — former San Cristóbal priest and UMAE organizer Archbishop Adolfo Suárez Rivera. As Ruiz met with Suárez Rivera and the CEM's twenty-one-member Permanent Council, Corripio and Salinas worked out details of a church-state peace initiative.

That evening, Salinas announced the forced resignation of his cousin, Interior Secretary and former governor of Chiapas González Garrido — the first time in modern memory that a president had directly sacked Mexico's number two political figure. Salinas substituted González Garrido with Jorge Carpizo, the former human rights ombudsman who had been unable to clean up drug-related corruption among federal police and prosecutors during his twelve-month tenure as attorney general. The president also resurrected from political oblivion Manuel Camacho — who by virtue of his public display of displeasure with Salinas's undemocratic choice of Colosio was the only PRI politico with any credibility left — naming his former confidant the government's "Commissioner for Peace and Reconciliation in Chiapas."

That same day, Camacho took care to phone Colosio in Sonora, where the PRI candidate was campaigning. Then, on January 11, Camacho met in the Mexico City archdiocesan curia with his second cousin by marriage — Archbishop Suárez Rivera — with Ruiz, Corripio, the CEM Permanent Council, and superiors of a dozen religious orders. The CEM unveiled a special bishops' commission on Chiapas, to include Ruiz, Suárez Rivera, and five other prelates. Then Ruiz and Camacho briefed reporters, while an Associated Press photographer snapped a telling picture of Camacho hugging Ruiz, with Cardinal Corripio hovering in the background.

By January 13, fighting in Chiapas had ground to a halt as the Zapatistas retreated to their stronghold near the remote town of Guadalupe Tepeyac. The truce prompted a reticent stock market recovery, and the next day Ruiz became official mediator between Camacho and the Zapatistas. Then Salinas offered the Zapatistas amnesty during a nationally televised address — inauspiciously delivered as he was seated beneath an oil portrait of ex-President Venustiano Carranza, the northern chieftain who had Emiliano Zapata murdered in 1919. Needless to say, the symbolism was not lost upon the neo-Zapatista leadership, nor on the public, who in the first days of fighting had seen televised images of poorly armed Mexican Indians heroically confronting a Mexican army given to brutal human rights abuse.

In a major public relations coup, the Zapatistas had wrested the banner of patriotism from the Mexican military, which since the revolution had embodied the spirit of nationalism and of *indigenismo*, being one of the few channels through which poor rural youth could "get ahead" in society. Tlatelolco and the 1970s "dirty war" against rural and urban insurgents were blots on the military's relatively professional record. But just prior to the rebellion its professionalism had come increasingly under fire: the bishops' CEPS commission had alleged a military–drug trafficking link; a "Commission of Truth" formed on the twenty-fifth anniversary of Tlatelolco revived memories of the army's role in the massacre; and the press took up the case of General José Francisco Gallardo, jailed for insubordination after he had dared acknowledge military human rights abuses.

The televised image of summarily executed Indian youth and reports of other army abuses so shocked many Mexicans that their loyalties shifted to the underdogs, the Zapatistas. When the fighting stopped, national newspapers ran eloquent communiqués from Subcomandante Marcos and the rebels' Indigenous Clandestine Revolutionary Committee (CCRI), further bolstering Zapatista support. At the forefront of solidarity was the Mexican human rights network, "All Rights for All," which organized international fact-finding missions to the conflict zones. Coordinating efforts with the San Cristóbal diocese's Fray Bartolomé center were the Dominicans' Fray Vitoria center and the Jesuits' Pro center in Mexico City. José Alvarez Icaza put CENCOS at the service of efforts to organize humanitarian aid, and when a video team sharing offices with CENCOS documented rights abuses in Chiapas, the center's offices were burglarized by unidentified persons on four occasions.

Weeks of public debate followed over whether the government's cease-fire and amnesty offers reflected President Salinas's "political will" to seek a peaceful solution, or simply a fear that the conflict could spread — dashing investor confidence and thereby wrecking NAFTA at the same time. But most commentators seemed to downplay the influence in the decision of two other major brokers: the church and the military — the "cross" and the "sword." Angry over being accused of war crimes after having done the dirty work for the politicians, the military high command was apparently unwilling to enter into a drawn-out, image-damaging conflict. The key may have been a division in the officer corps, with regular army officers resentful over the privilege enjoyed by their colleagues of the Presidential Guard (EMP). That former EMP commander Godínez Bravo was neither able to abort the rebellion nor stop the Zapatistas from overrunning the Rancho Nuevo perimeter confirmed to regular army that the EMP was full of "velvet soldiers."[24]

Uneasy Negotiations

The Catholic hierarchy also realized that a counterinsurgency war in Chiapas could lead to the kind of repression against the church that occurred in the 1980s in neighboring Central America. As with the military, the rebellion also served to highlight divisions in the church's "high command." On January 15, two top Corripio advisors — Fathers González Torres and Roqueñi — met with Prigione and demanded he tender his resignation, saying his activities had become harmful to the Mexican church. Cardinal Corripio later denied prior knowledge of the two priests' visit to Prigione, but Roqueñi claimed the cardinal had given his tacit blessing, saying "go see him [Prigione] and tell him whatever you have to tell him."[25]

The dispute was further complicated by revelations that the Jesuit order and indigenous communities in Chihuahua state's Tarahumara region were upset with the Vatican's choice of an urban diocesan priest from another state to replace the late Bishop José Llaguno. Not only was the new bishop unfamiliar with local indigenous people, but Prigione had counselled the Vatican to move the diocesan see to the only non-indigenous town in the region — an untimely decision, given the discrimination against Indians that had fueled the Chiapas crisis. The besieged Vatican envoy rebounded, however, with the aid of Archbishop Suárez Rivera and the emergence of the bishops' special commission on Chiapas. After a two-day commission visit to Chiapas, Prigione accompanied commission members on January 15 to visit Attorney General Carpizo, speaking afterwards of Samuel Ruiz's peace-mediating role in near-laudatory terms.

On January 21, Suárez Rivera made clear in presenting the bishops' first report on Chiapas that "marginalization, hunger, and poverty suffered by the poor of the Chiapas highlands"[26] was at the root of the conflict. But the CEM president also backed Prigione, calling demands for the Vatican envoy's ouster "very irresponsible." Reiterating that support in a memo to Mexican bishops and religious superiors, Suárez Rivera provoked the ire of Catholic activists. During a forum on religious freedom at the Universidad Iberoamericana on January 29–30, dozens of Catholic activists and church-linked organizations called for canon lawyers to investigate Prigione's comportment and later issued a letter of their own, demanding that the Vatican's pro-nuncio "terminate his duties in our country."

Stock market speculation soared as special government envoy Manuel Camacho received a first message via Bishop Ruiz from the Zapatista leadership in Chiapas, saying they were willing to discuss the terms of negotiations. Yet news that the Mexican Congress had passed Salinas's amnesty law prompted Marcos to ask rhetorically in an open letter, "For what do we have to ask pardon? For what will they pardon us? For not having died of hunger? For not having kept quiet about our misery?"[27] Camacho replied honestly that "nobody can place themselves above anybody else to grant pardon, when so many things have happened during so many years that never should have happened."[28] As messages went in and out of the jungle, the Fray Bartolomé center further angered the military by revealing the gruesome murder of three Tzeltal men from the Morelia ejido, near Altamirano, whose mutilated remains were found February 11 after having last been reported seen in the custody of army troops.

The bishops' commission visited Chiapas again in late January, denouncing that relief aid was being conditioned upon support for the military, with poor Indians forced to participate in demonstrations against the Zapatistas and Bishop Ruiz. On their third visit, the bishops felt compelled to intercede in Altamirano for the embattled Sisters of Charity, who were daily being threatened with expulsion by mobs incited by cattle ranchers and business owners. In San Cristóbal, the bishops' commission also observed the government-rebel dialogue taking place in the cathedral. On February 20, amid great public expectation fomented by the presence of four hundred Mexican and foreign journalists, nineteen Zapatista delegates arrived under escort to the cathedral, refurbished for the government-rebel "dialogue" and rechristened by Bishop Ruiz the "Cathedral of Peace." Indigenous in the majority, wearing their native dress and concealing their identities with ski masks, the Zapatista delegates included a dozen members of the rebels' political directorate and seven military commanders, including the ubiquitous Subcomandante Marcos.

The talks lasted eight days until finally a list of thirty-two government "Commitments for Peace," corresponding to thirty-four original Zapatista demands, were revealed to the press. It was not a "peace accord," as such, a development that damped national optimism and again sent the volatile stock market spiraling downward. The majority of the demands were for resolution of specific socio-economic and political ills, to which Camacho responded with concrete proposals. But the government's peace commissioner secured only vague promises from Salinas regarding two key rebel demands: for "truly free and democratic elections" and for "resignation of the titular head of the federal Executive [branch]."[29] With the unresolved questions of democracy and upcoming national elections looming large, the Zapatistas retired to the jungle to consult their indigenous supporters on the government's offer.

Clearly, Salinas did not intend to resign, and confusion surrounded the election process over speculation that Salinas might jettison Colosio as PRI candidate, replacing him with the now immensely popular Camacho. Overshadowed after New Year's Day by the Zapatista rebellion, Colosio had done everything to raise his standings in the polls. He had tried to shake the perception that he was Salinas's puppet, bowing to opposition demands to sign a joint document called "Twenty Commitments to Democracy," designed to guarantee free and fair elections. On March 6, during a sixty-fifth anniversary celebration of the PRI, he shocked the party old guard by embracing the opposition's call for the PRI's "independence with respect to the government."[30]

Colosio had even expressed solidarity with Camacho's peace efforts, but after the conspicuous absence of both Salinas and Camacho from the PRI celebration, on March 10 — as the mysterious kidnapping of banker Alfredo Harp Helú sent the Mexican stock market into a tailspin — Colosio went on the attack against his rival. Camacho had studiously avoided ruling out a run for the presidency, and it was becoming clear that the Zapatistas' consultation process might drag on for weeks, with no peace accord in immediate sight. Even with political bickering in the PRD undermining the candidacy of Cuauhtemoc Cárdenas and PAN candidate Diego Fernández becoming all but irrelevant, Colosio was having trouble raising his standing in the polls above 44 percent.

Despite the Colosio-Camacho feuding, optimism and the stock market began to rise with the prospect that fair elections might be held for the first time since 1912. Even the notion that free elections might resolve the Zapatista crisis and put Mexico firmly on the road to democracy was not enough to convince investors, however; as the end of March approached, it was clear that the rate of foreign investment was slowing markedly while domestic investors had pulled their capital out of Mexico to the tune of $5.2 billion.[31] Indeed, there was room for caution, and Bishop Ruiz — now receiving death threats, while his diocesan team was daily the target of threats and demonstrations promoted by the local elite — warned that the political confusion surrounding the Camacho-Colosio dispute and pressure being exerted on the Zapatistas to conclude their consultation could undermine the peace process. Given the circumstances, and with a special congressional session set for the week of March 22 to discuss further electoral reform, Camacho withdrew himself from the presidential running, saying that "above any [personal] aspiration is my decision to guide the peace process in Chiapas."[32]

Colosio's relief and praise for Camacho was immediate, but within twenty-four hours it was violently, tragically cut short: during a March 23 campaign rally in the Tijuana shantytown of Lomas Taurinas, the PRI candidate was assassinated in cold blood. Consecutive shock waves ran through Mexico's economy and society amid conflictive reports as to whether the gunman acted alone or in concert with members of Colosio's own security detail and Baja California state PRI party members. Questions arose as to how the assassin could have penetrated the candidate's security, headed up by General Domiro García Reyes, former chief aide to General Godínez Bravo in the Presidential Guard and the same officer who coordinated John Paul II's security during the 1990 papal visit. Ire among the general public and PRI faithful turned on Camacho, who was jeered as he arrived to pay his respects as Colosio's body lay in state at Mexico City PRI headquarters. Salinas promised a full investigation, but then lost credibility by assigning as special prosecutor Miguel Montes, the PRI congressman who had railroaded Salinas's ratification as president-elect through the Chamber of Deputies in 1988. With the murder of Cardinal Posadas in 1993 still shrouded in mystery, the public was disinclined to believe the truth would ever be known about the Colosio killing.

7

Elections and Choices:
Church, Society, and the Future

L IKE THE NATION in general, the Catholic hierarchy was shocked by Colosio's assassination. In the victim's home state of Sonora, Archbishop Carlos Quintero Arce called the murder "totally reprehensible" and said that the church had high hopes that Colosio would have worked "above all, to help the neediest, to eradicate poverty, [and] to increase the salaries of workers."[1] Archbishop Suárez Rivera expressed "great pain and sadness"[2] from Monterrey, while in Mexico City the CEM's general secretary, Auxiliary Bishop Ramón Godínez of Guadalajara, called the murder an attempt to destabilize the nation. In San Cristóbal, Bishop Ruiz clearly sensed the danger of the situation, hoping beyond hope that as a result of the murder "the peace and dialogue process with the EZLN has not suffered any change."[3]

As the Zapatista forces went on maximum alert, the only negotiations taking place were between the PRI old guard and the Salinista technocrats over a possible successor to Colosio. Potential candidates included the colorless party president Francisco Ortiz Arana and former Guerrero state Governor José Francisco Ruiz Massieu, an ex-brother-in-law of Salinas, who took himself out of the running on March 27 to avoid charges of nepotism. Two days later, Ortiz Arana withdrew and Salinas settled on Colosio's campaign manager and former Secretary of Planning and Budget and Secretary of Education, Ernesto Zedillo.

Like most of the technocrats, Zedillo had never held elective office, but his past was unprecedented for a PRI candidate. While the center-left PRD's Cárdenas had spent his privileged childhood in the National Palace, Zedillo grew up in poverty in the Pueblo Nuevo shantytown in the northern border city of Mexicali, where he worked selling newspapers and shining shoes as a child. He later attended a vocational high school in Mexico City, and then worked part-time while attending the National Polytechnic Institute. It was only by virtue of winning a U.S. government scholarship that he was able to attend Yale, where he earned a doctorate in economics.

The choice of Zedillo pleased many bishops, and not only because he had been an altar boy, belonged to a Catholic youth group, and remembered with fondness the parish priest of his Pueblo Nuevo childhood. Even more so than in Colosio's case, the CEM leadership thought that, if elected, Zedillo's past would make him a more sympathetic president, that the poverty of his youth would help to narrow the chasm separating Mexico's poor and powerful.[4]

In the days and weeks after the Colosio killing, a climate of confusion and fear was fueled by revelations that pointed to conspiracy — perhaps even one hatched from within the ruling party. In the midst of the turmoil, the Catholic hierarchy seemed convinced that Zedillo and the PRI would respect Colosio's commitment to fair elections. In the interim between the Zapatista rebellion and the Colosio murder, the sixteen-member CEM Permanent Council had issued a pastoral letter that spoke of the "painful" reality of Mexico's "not yet having attained credibility in election results" and called for the upcoming August 21 elections to be held in a spirit of "truth, generating participation, respect for the act of voting, and engendering the justice that is the basis of lasting peace."[5] After Colosio's killing, on April 15, the full membership of the CEM issued another letter, calling for Mexicans to work together to ensure free elections and rejecting violent post-electoral protest, but still leaving the door open to "passive resistance" as a means of ensuring respect for the vote outcome.[6]

Zedillo seemed intent on respecting Colosio's promise of change — he referred to his predecessor nearly forty times in his March 29 acceptance speech for the candidacy — but his room to maneuver was limited. Apparently as a concession to the PRI dinosaurs, the very next day Salinas sent the architect of his neo-liberal economic program, top advisor José María Córdoba Montoya, into virtual exile as Mexico's representative to the Inter-American Development Bank. A cryptic figure who rarely appeared in public, the French-born Córdoba was blamed in his role as national security advisor for allowing the Zapatista rebellion and the Colosio murder to occur. A key supporter of Zedillo's candidacy, it was apparently feared by some within the party that Córdoba exercised undue influence over the new PRI candidate.

Many observers saw other signs that the PRI's political dinosaur cartel was making a comeback: while evoking Colosio's memory to win the "sympathy vote," Zedillo nevertheless balked before signing the "Twenty Commitments toward Democracy" document — Colosio's signing of the document was said to have upset party hard-liners. Then, in short order, reports began to circulate of a major party leadership shakeup that would return to power a faction of the old guard, led by millionaire-politician Carlos Hank González. A former schoolteacher who had made a fortune in and out of politics, the gray-haired and gnarly faced Hank was the political guru of the Atlacomulco

Group of México state PRI politicians. In the 1970s, he had been México state governor, and then Mexico City mayor during the corruption-tainted administration of López Portillo. In 1988, Salinas appointed him Secretary of Tourism and, later, Secretary of Agriculture and Water Resources. The apparent pact between technocrats and dinosaurs was said to guarantee continuation of Salinas's economic reforms through a Zedillo presidency, while relinquishing political control to the old guard via Hank. Indeed, Hank loyalist Humberto Benítez Treviño had already assumed control of the Mexico City district attorney's office. And, it seemed imminent that Hank lieutenant José Ignacio Pichardo Pagaza would become the next PRI party president.[7]

At the same time, press revelations that the Mexican military was importing anti-riot tanks in apparent anticipation of post-electoral protest sent a chill of fear across the country. A second kidnapping of a top Mexican businessman on April 26 coincided with the Salinas-decreed creation of an all-powerful National Security Council, stifling an improvement on the national barometer of well-being, the stock market. In Chiapas, after a hiatus caused by the Colosio murder, the Zapatistas renewed their consultation process, but it became increasingly apparent that something had gone awry. While both Camacho and Bishop Ruiz repeatedly told the press that a second and conclusive round of the talks seemed imminent, instead of confirmation that the Zapatistas might be near acceptance of the government's peace offer there was an ominous silence coming from the jungle.

Pre-election Jitters

Taking advantage of a temporary lull, in late April Bishop Ruiz wrote to Cardinal Roger Etchegaray, president of the Pontifical Council for Justice and Peace, to see if he might speak in Rome on the situation in Chiapas during a justice and peace conference in May. After receiving an affirmative response, Ruiz dispatched as an advance team his new legal counsel, Father Roqueñi, along with lay Catholic Miguel Alvarez, nephew of CENCOS director José Alvarez Icaza. Once in Rome, the two made appointments for Ruiz with other Vatican officials, and on May 6 Ruiz left Mexico City for the Vatican. In fact, the trip was largely a lobbying effort to bolster the bishop's position vis-à-vis the still-pending charges against him by the Congregation for Bishops. Roqueñi was to assess the legal case against Ruiz, while Alvarez acted as press and public relations liaison. Bishop Ruiz was unsuccessful in his attempt to meet with Pope John Paul II, who was convalescing from recent hip surgery. But the visit did seem to level the playing field for Ruiz in his struggle with Prigione, except for the fact that it played less well back home, where the news magazine *Proceso* caught Alvarez putting too much "spin" on a questionable version of the visit, which had it that Vatican officials had criticized Prigione during discussions with Ruiz.[8]

While Bishop Ruiz was still in Rome, Mexico's presidential candidates held the country's first-ever televised political debates, which proved a turning point in the presidential campaign. PAN candidate Diego Fernández, a polished trial lawyer and skillful orator, wiped the floor with both his opponents — lashing out at Cárdenas's undemocratic past as a former PRI senator and governor and destroying Zedillo with an exposé of the Salinistas' poor democratic and mixed economic track record. The debate sent Fernández's public image soaring: more than 45 percent of those who viewed the debate thought the PAN candidate won, and within two days a national survey showed Fernández preferred by 37 percent of Mexicans, with Zedillo second at 26 percent and Cárdenas a distant third with just 8 percent.

The next day, the shift in political power toward the dinosaurs was consummated with the swearing in of Pichardo Pagaza as PRI president and Benítez Treviño as federal attorney general. Apparently to balance the influence of the Hank group, Salinas appointed his former brother-in-law and confidant, José Francisco Ruiz Massieu, to the key post of PRI general secretary. Ruiz Massieu soon spoke out in favor of democratic reforms of the party and the country, in the spirit of Colosio. A balance to Benítez Treviño, Ruiz Massieu's brother, Mario, a Salinas loyalist and holdover from Jorge Carpizo's twelve-month stint in the top law enforcement post, stayed on as assistant attorney general and took charge of the Posadas and other drug-related cases.

With fear and uncertainty among the public over what calamity might next occur on the road to the August 21 elections, tension mounted in Chiapas as mestizo and indigenous campesinos, emboldened by the Zapatista rebellion, staged land takeovers, and the thirty-year-old conflict that had seen twenty thousand Tzotzil Evangelicals expelled from Chamula flared into violence. As the PRD and PRI candidates for the Chiapas governorship geared up their campaigns, the Zapatistas' consultation process dragged on while the literary Subcomandante Marcos increasingly threatened in open letters that there would be civil war nationwide should national elections be anything but pristine.

Clearly, the rebel leadership were setting themselves up as moral arbiters of Mexico's political future, a situation made very clear when Marcos dealt a severe blow to Cárdenas's image by upbraiding the PRD for the same "vices that have poisoned the party in power."[9] In the run-up to the balloting, the Zapatistas then dropped a political bombshell: on June 12, the national press reproduced four rebel communiqués in which the Zapatista leadership rejected the government's response to their demands. They declared the peace dialogue terminated and offered rebel-held territory to independent activists and NGOs as a site for a "National Democratic Convention," out of which a transitional government was to arise, "either through the resignation of the federal Executive [Salinas de Gortari] or through the electoral process."[10] Zedillo immediately criticized Camacho for having failed to broker a peaceful settlement and for repeatedly assuring the public that peace was at hand. The show of no-confidence from the man who seemed the probable next president left Camacho little choice but to resign — chastising Zedillo and PRI as he did so for what he called their growing intolerance

Anti-Church Campaign

The recourse to violence, the polarization, suspicion, and intolerance taking over Mexican society had a definite effect on the Catholic Church hierarchy. Sources close to the bishops say they began to focus their attention not on democracy or social justice, but on the need to maintain "social peace" in the face of a deteriorating situation. The downward spiral since January certainly showed signs of affecting the church directly. The campaign against the San Cristóbal diocese had assumed national implications, with the Televisa-owned financial daily *Summa* charging the Jesuits with subversion nationwide. In July, prominent Jesuits joined provincial superior Jesús Morales Orozco in denouncing a "campaign orchestrated by right-wing groups, among both the general public and within the government,"[11] aimed at forcing a Jesuit retreat from their commitment to social justice. Not only had Televisa-owned media accused several Jesuits of being Subcomandante Marcos, but the national magazine *Impacto* accused Jesuit rights activists in Chihuahua state of supporting a non-existent "Chihuahua Armed Command" guerrilla group. There were also raids by armed men on a Jesuit social assistance center in Chiapas and on their De Colores retreat house near Acapulco, the latter following misleading local news reports that Jesuit Father Jesús Maldonado had been training guerrillas there. In fact, Maldonado had conducted a workshop in late June for poll watchers for the upcoming elections.

That seminar was held as part of the activities of the umbrella pro-democracy organization, Civic Alliance, of which the Jesuits' Miguel A. Pro human rights center and other Mexican NGOs were affiliates. Formed in 1992 and partly funded by the U.S. National Endowment for Democracy, the Civic Alliance was monitoring the campaigns and training volunteers to watch polls on August 21. While the church hierarchy organized its own poll-watching apparatus through the CEPS commission, a large number of

Catholic social activists joined the Civic Alliance efforts as individuals or groups. In fact, by election time nearly a quarter of the estimated twenty-one thousand Civic Alliance volunteers nationwide came "from Catholic youth organizations, the basic Christian community movement, and religious orders — seminarians, priests and nuns."[12] Rogelio Gómez Hermosillo, longtime CEBs advisor and ecumenical activist, was on the national Coordinating Council; ten of thirty-two Civic Alliance state coordinators were CEBs activists, and two more state representatives were priests — Jesuit Father Francisco Goitia in Tabasco state and diocesan Father Fidencio González in Nayarit state.

That the series of attacks on the Jesuits might be part of a campaign to undermine the church's moral voice by associating it with leftist guerrillas was not acknowledged by the hierarchy. But any doubts they might have had were soon dispelled. In May, newly installed archbishop of Guadalajara Juan Sandoval Iñiguez made a high-profile appeal for Guadalajarans to come forward anonymously and provide the local church with any information that might help to solve the case of Cardinal Posadas's murder. Showing the same independence from Prigione and the CEM leadership that earlier had led him to caution colleagues about church-state coziness, Sandoval stepped on the government's toes by affirming that law enforcement officials had told him that up to 40 percent of federal judicial police were in league with drug traffickers.

Whether or not the Jesuits were correct that a campaign was being waged against them from within the government is unclear. But attacks against individuals and religious orders soon escalated into attacks against the church in general. On July 7, while a second of three groups of Mexican bishops was at the Vatican for their *ad limina* visits, General Ramón Mota Sánchez, an army officer and former Mexico City police chief-turned-politician, charged that funds from the German Catholic development agencies Misereor and Adveniat had been channelled through the San Cristóbal diocese to the Zapatista rebels. The source is what made the charges serious, given that Mota Sánchez was an important PRI member of the Chamber of Deputies' National Defense Committee. With Bishop Ruiz at the Vatican for his uneventful *ad limina* visit, the charges were rebutted by San Cristóbal diocesan spokespersons as well as the German embassy in Mexico. The Mexican hierarchy, most of whom at one time or another had received funding from the German church agencies, were angered by the attack and perceived the charges as a direct affront to the integrity of the universal church.

The cooling of church-government relations became absolutely evident shortly thereafter, when it became known in the Guadalajara archdiocese that as a result of an appeal by Archbishop Sandoval, a half-dozen eyewitnesses to the Posadas murder had come forward on the condition that they could remain anonymous. Confidential Guadalajara church sources say that some of the witnesses were members of a group of Jehovah's Witnesses who had been proselytizing daily in the Guadalajara airport and were present the entire day of the cardinal's killing. After Archbishop Prigione's flight from Mexico to Guadalajara was already in the air, about two hours before the cardinal arrived, the witnesses observed that an unusually large number of police arrived at the airport, thinking in hindsight that it was "as if they were waiting for him" to arrive. When the cardinal's Grand Marquis pulled up outside the airport terminal, the archdiocesan sources quoted the witnesses as saying that the gunmen went straight to the vehicle and opened fire in a "direct attack" on Posadas.

Although Archbishop Sandoval had been invited by law enforcement authorities to present any evidence he thought relevant in the case, he was rebuffed after he turned over the testimonies to the attorney general's office. In a press conference on August 4, Assistant Attorney General Mario Ruiz Massieu dismissed the testimony as useless and cautioned Sandoval to "abstain from making absolutely baseless and frivolous statements."[13] Stung by Ruiz Massieu's remarks, Sandoval and the hierarchy chose not to press their case because a parallel development had put them in a difficult position.

On July 26, the national daily *Excélsior* began a three-part series in which it was revealed that the two top suspects in the Posadas murder, Ramón and Benjamín Arellano Félix, had met eight months earlier on two separate occasions with none other than Archbishop Prigione in the Vatican pro-nuncio's Mexico City residence. The Arellano Félix brothers set up the meetings through a Tijuana diocesan priest, Father Gerardo Montaño. Ordained in 1978 by then-Bishop Posadas of Tijuana, Father Montaño had been placed by Posadas in charge of the huge fund-raising effort for the construction of the Tijuana seminary, and his association with the Arellano Félix clan is believed to have dated to that period.

Father Montaño alleged that prior to the Prigione-Arellano Félix meetings he personally delivered to the pro-nuncio sealed envelopes addressed to Pope John Paul II.[14] In the *Excélsior* series, the drug lords gave alibis to show they were in Tijuana at the time of the killing, and it was revealed that Prigione had left Ramón Arellano Félix at his residence while he went personally to discuss the brothers' claims of innocence with President Salinas and then Interior Secretary González Garrido.

For eight months, while all Mexico's law enforcement authorities were reportedly hunting for the fugitive drug traffickers, neither Prigione nor Salinas nor González Garrido ever revealed that the meetings took place. But on July 27 Prigione felt obliged to issue a four-point "clarification," admitting to having met with the Arellano Félix brothers to discuss "personal matters" and that, contrary to their claim, he did not administer the sacrament of absolution. Unable to evoke the secret of confession, Prigione nonetheless said he would "maintain professional secrecy" about the topic of discussion. Since the two admitted no guilt, Prigione said, he advised them to turn themselves in to authorities.[15] Archbishop Sandoval seemed immediately irritated, but the CEM leadership closed ranks quickly to support Prigione.

While media allegations of church-guerrilla links had undermined the church's authority to pronounce on Chiapas, the leak of the Prigione-Arellano Félix meetings likewise undercut its authority to condemn drug trafficking and corruption. At the same time, the hierarchy's position on the elections was also weakened with a front-page *Excélsior* banner headline on the third day of the Prigione series blaring: "Plan for Violence in 12 States; Includes Priests and Guerrillas."[16] The story was a rehash of the allegations that subversion was planned at the Jesuits' poll-watching workshop near Acapulco. Suspiciously, there were no sources to corroborate outrageous charges of alleged church plans for post-election terrorism contained in the story — obviously, it was a "plant."

Six days later, the CEM Permanent Council issued the bishops' third joint pastoral letter of the year on democracy and violence.[17] Picking up on a papal theme of "reconciliation" from their *ad limina* visits in July, the bishops' call for unity and order was standard fare — the exception being one paragraph in which they gave their blessing to what they said they felt was a "reliable" voter registration list. At the time, a debate raged over the credibility of the voter rolls, manipulated in past elections in favor of the PRI. While the PAN had said it believed the registration lists adequate, the PRD was claiming that thousands of its supporters had been "shaved" from the lists. What methodology — if any — the hierarchy used to analyze the reliability of the voter rolls is uncertain. But the message was very clear: in throwing its support along with the PAN to the government over this crucial point, the hierarchy was letting it be known that the PRD could not count on their support in the event of an electoral dispute.

Election Day and the Aftermath

As the elections drew near, Zedillo had moved back into the lead after Fernández's campaign stagnated; Cárdenas, meanwhile, appeared to be gaining ground in a repeat of 1988. In Chiapas, delegates to a Zapatista-convened National Democratic Convention (CND) on August 6–9 discussed Mexico's post-electoral future, with CENCOS director and CND Vice-President José

Alvarez Icaza telling the press that the CND would opt for "civil insurgence" in the event of electoral fraud in favor of the PRI.[18] Clear warnings to church activists began to appear: on August 7, posters bearing death threats to Jesuits were pasted outside half a dozen of the order's residences and centers in Mexico City and Puebla. At the same time, Civic Alliance activists began to complain of surveillance and harassment. But the Jesuits and the thousands of lay Catholic activists working with the Civic Alliance election monitoring campaign were not so easily intimidated.

With broadcasting coverage of the campaign slanted toward PRI candidate Zedillo and with the Civic Alliance signaling irregularities in the voter rolls, the independent vote-monitoring group issued a critical review just two days before the balloting: although the election might prove to be "relatively credible," Civic Alliance said that in-built bias in the electoral process would make it neither "equitable nor reliable."[19] Right up to election eve — with the PRI's campaign slogan of "For the Good of Your Family: Ernesto Zedillo" sounding more like a threat than a promise — government-sponsored radio ad campaigns raised the specter of post-electoral violence and chaos.

As the polls opened on August 21, long lines signalled a massive voter turnout, and by the time the polls closed an estimated 75 percent of the country's 45 million voters had cast ballots. Remarkable was the absence of massive, at-the-ballot-box fraud. Official returns showed Zedillo with 50 percent, Diego Fernández coming in second with 26 percent, and Cuauhtemoc Cárdenas a distant third, at 17 percent. What analysts called the "fear vote" was decisive, along with a myriad of "irregularities" occurring in remote rural areas of states like Chiapas, Oaxaca, and Guerrero — where campesino and indigenous communities were reportedly compelled to swap their votes for PROCAMPO payments and other social benefits. Scores of independent foreign observers agreed with the assessment of Father Fidencio González, Nayarit state Civic Alliance coordinator, that there may have been "a big vote in favor of the dominant party [PRI], but it was the result of pressure and coercion."[20]

Withholding judgment until its poll-watching data was collected, the Civic Alliance eventually concluded that the number of votes tallied generally corresponded to votes cast, but that multiple irregularities made the electoral process far from fair. An eighty-member team from the U.S.-based National Democratic Institute, the National Republican Institute and the Carter Center approved the voting almost immediately. Likewise, the Mexican bishops deemed the IFE's preliminary returns "reliable" within forty-eight hours, basing its assessment largely on limited information from 2,320 church observers in a scant eighteen of the country's seventy-nine Catholic dioceses.

Some Catholic activists were disillusioned with the hierarchy's response.

Alvarez Icaza claimed that CND members throughout the country "saw the fraud occur...[and] we're asking for the annulment of the elections." A team of observers fielded by the Mexico City archdiocesan human rights office felt cheated, said office director María Teresa Jardi, having been "led to believe that the elections would be impeccable, and they weren't." Civic Alliance leader Gómez Hermosillo charged that the hierarchy's quick reaction was because it owed the government a favor because of the 1992 repeal of anti-church measures in the constitution. The bishops, said Gómez, "did not want to see any figures that did not confirm their wishes" for a PRI-government victory — a charge to which CEM General Secretary Godínez responded that "recognition of the church had nothing to do with it.... That's how we saw the situation."[21]

In direct contrast to 1988, Cárdenas's call for nationwide protests fizzled in the face of an obvious Zedillo majority, as did the CND threat of "civil insurgence." With the PRI winning not only the presidency but clear majorities in both houses of Congress, the expected continuation of the Salinista economic program for another presidential term reassured Mexican and foreign private investors. But no sooner had the PRI election euphoria subsided than drug-related scandals began to erode government credibility.

First, former 1968 student leader and ex-journalist Eduardo Valle publicly charged that Mexico's Gulf coast drug cartel had infiltrated the Colosio campaign and may have been linked to his assassination. According to Valle, who had been hired as a federal prosecutor by ex-Attorney General Carpizo to investigate a series of drug-cartel killings of Mexican journalists, the Gulf cartel was transporting cocaine for Colombia's Cali drug cartel to the U.S. market and had worrisome links with at least two top Salinas administration officials — Secretary of Communications and Transportation Emilio Gamboa and former Salinas chief of staff, Córdoba Montoya. The revelations sparked renewed talk of conspiracy in Colosio's death and of a link with the Posadas murder.

Then in September, prompted by U.S. Treasury Secretary Lloyd Bentsen to crack down on drug-money laundering, the Mexican Treasury Secretariat moved against multibillionaire Carlos Cabal Peniche for alleged illegal lending practices within his business and banking empire. It was also revealed that the U.S. Drug Enforcement Administration (DEA) had been investigating Cabal — who had mysteriously made his entire fortune in the few short years that Carlos Salinas had been in office — for possible links to the Cali cartel. The church was immersed in the scandal with revelations that a French-born Marist priest, Father Jacques Charveriat, had sat on the boards of Cabal's Banco Cremi-Union and his Florida-based Del Monte Fresh Produce company. A member of a wealthy vintner family from Lyons, France,

Charveriat was apparently providing spiritual and financial counsel to Cabal and other Mexican businessmen in exchange for philanthropic donations to various charities that he ran. Still, the church connection revived fresh memories of the Prigione-Arellano Félix meetings and generated more embarrassing speculation that the church might be involved in what some came to call "alms laundering."

Such were minor scandals for the PRI government compared to the September 28 assassination of PRI General Secretary José Francisco Ruiz Massieu, which cut short the hopes for a smooth presidential transition. Ruiz Massieu was apparently the linchpin in a Salinas-Zedillo strategy for gradual democratization of both the ruling party and Mexico's electoral system. The murder left the PRI bereft of one of its top strategists and was a direct blow to Salinas, who as the uncle of Ruiz Massieu's eldest child was extremely close to his family. Assistant Attorney General Mario Ruiz Massieu, the victim's brother, accepted assignment to the case and followed the murder trail to PRI politicians from the northern border state of Tamaulipas, the home base of the Gulf cartel denounced by former prosecutor Valle. Involvement by PRI politicians, the Gulf coast connection, and Mario Ruiz Massieu's admission of "common denominators" in the Posadas, Colosio, and Ruiz Massieu murders[22] pointed to a possible long-term political conspiracy with involvement by drug traffickers.

In the midst of the turmoil, Mexico's attention again turned to Chiapas, as the Zapatistas broke off preliminary negotiations with Camacho's replacement, new peace envoy Jorge Madrazo. The surprise announcement came as the CND was holding a second assembly in San Cristóbal to discuss future actions in solidarity with the Zapatistas' demands for social justice. The rebel announcement caused Bishop Ruiz to cancel a scheduled trip abroad and to launch a new peace initiative, which included a National Mediating Commission (CONAI) comprised of eight individuals. The move got a mixed reaction from Madrazo, who failed to meet even once with the rebels during his four months in the post. Announcing that the government accepted Ruiz's proposal that the army pull back to positions in Chiapas held prior to Colosio's murder, Madrazo rejected the idea of the commission, saying the government had not been consulted ahead of time by Ruiz.

The move fueled speculation that the Chiapas bishop might be preparing to step down as sole mediator, especially given press leaks out of Rome in September that the Vatican's Congregation for Bishops again intended to push for Ruiz's removal as San Cristóbal's bishop. In Mexico City, church sources said Prigione had been about to read a second letter from Cardinal Gantin to Ruiz — until the pro-nuncio left for Italy and his annual September holidays. It was widely believed that during his stay in Rome, Prigione discussed not only Ruiz's position, but also two situations critical to the future of Mexico's Catholic Church.

In June, Cardinal Corripio had submitted his mandatory resignation at age seventy-five to the pope and, while Prigione was at the Vatican, on September 28 John Paul accepted the resignation. Mexico City's auxiliary bishops immediately voted to make Corripio temporary administrator of the megalithic archdiocese until a successor was chosen. Vatican and archdiocesan officials had let it be known that Corripio's successor would enjoy far less power than had the cardinal; in keeping with the pope's longtime wish to divide the archdiocese, four new dioceses were to be created in the Valley of Mexico, while the reduced archdiocese would be allowed to retain the Basilica of Guadalupe.

Not only was the Vatican of John Paul II thus positioned to name a new primate cardinal for Mexico City — in addition to a second cardinal to fill the vacancy left by Posadas's murder — but four new appointee bishops from greater Mexico City were added to the ranks of the CEM. At the same time, Prigione returned to Mexico in late October to attend the semi-annual CEM assembly, all important because of the selection of a successor for Suárez Rivera as CEM president. Had he lived, Cardinal Posadas would have been an obvious candidate, but in his absence, the field was limited and the bishop's preferences unclear.

Some observers believed that although Prigione held important influence within the hierarchy, having overseen appointment of fifty-two of eighty-eight Mexican bishops as of the October 1994 CEM election, there might be a backlash within the bishops conference to his constant — and sometimes un-wanted — presence in Mexican church affairs. Had there been a general back-lash against Prigione, the bishops might have chosen two Prigione appointees who had nevertheless shown their independence from the pro-nuncio in re-cent months, Archbishops Héctor González and Juan Sandoval. On the other hand, some observers believed Prigione loyalists and more traditionalist bish-ops might opt in the CEM presidential election for a low-profile figure, one who had shown himself to be a good administrator and who did not rock the boat — like the quiet but competent Archbishop Rosendo Huesca of Puebla or the coadjutor-turned-archbishop of Chihuahua, José Fernández Arteaga.

The Church and the Uncertain Future

As the CEM assembly approached, Prigione returned to Mexico with a sur-prise announcement that the Vatican would soon be naming a team of apostolic visitors to visit Mexico's religious orders, with whom Prigione had experienced some difficulty since the Zapatista uprising. The Mexican Catholic hierarchy had come to an uneasy understanding with Mexico's religious orders since an awkward period in 1989–91, when the Vatican cracked down on the Latin American Confederation of Religious (CLAR), canceling an allegedly "ideologized and reductionist" pastoral program and hand-picking the organization's leadership. In Mexico, it was accepted that the religious orders had a different "charisma" than did the institutional church,[23] giving them greater freedom of action — as long as their activities did not cause undue embarrassment or difficulties for the hierarchy. But the increased activism in the area of human rights and social justice — particularly from within Mexico's Dominican and Jesuit provinces — had often run counter to the hierarchy's attempts to smooth over relations with the government. Moreover, the fact that the Dominicans had chosen outspoken human rights activist Miguel Concha as their provincial superior, the Dominican and Jesuit roles in Chiapas and the pressure exercised against Prigione since January by Jesuit González Torres and the order's Tarahumara community had certainly not pleased the Vatican delegate.

Archbishop Prigione bore no immediate word regarding Samuel Ruiz, however, and the Chiapas bishop dedicated himself to firming up the CONAI in the midst of growing tension in the southern state. At the same time, he prepared to attend the CEM's semi-annual assembly in Cuernavaca, the diocese of Prigione stalwart Luis Reynoso Cervantes, who promised a gala celebration of the inauguration of luxurious new seminary facilities to commemorate a hundred years of the founding of the diocesan seminary. Ruiz arrived with the same bodyguard provided him since January by the Interior Secretariat, only this time dressed as an unlikely Cuernavaca diocesan seminarian. He shunned media attention, hoping to avoid even more controversy and notoriety, something he knew that most of his fellow bishops — whose support he could not afford to lose — detested almost above all else.

After three days of debate and discussion, it was time for the Mexican bishops to elect a new set of four officers to the presidency of the CEM. Well-placed sources within the bishops' conference said the race was the "most hard-fought" they had ever seen. All depended upon whether or not "Prigione is able to impose his will on the bishops," said the source. There was an unusual delay in the regular noon press conference on October 27, at which bishops from northern Mexico were slated to issue a critical statement regarding California's pending Proposition 187 ballot measure, deemed racist and discriminatory against Hispanics by bishops on both sides of the U.S.-Mexico border. As Bishops Carlos Quintero Arce, José Ulises Macías of Mexicali, and Emilio Berlie of Tijuana arrived for the conference, they had a surprise with them: not only would CEM spokesman Reynoso attend, but they were also accompanied by former two-term CEM president Archbishop Sergio Obeso Rivera of Xalapa.

A prelate who knew how to negotiate with the government — having "cultivated the ground"[24] in the mid-1980s for eventual church-state talks that led to the legal recognition of the Mexican church in 1992 — yet who supported the CEBs movement in his archdiocese and spoke out decidedly on social issues, the sixty-three-year-old archbishop had been elected as a compromise choice and "unity candidate"[25] to a third term as CEM president. Speaking at the press conference, the fair-skinned and balding Obeso squinted in the glare of television cameras as he alluded to the recent assassinations and the Chiapas uprising in telling reporters that the Mexican church needs to "face up to the violence that has manifested itself in various ways recently. . . . As a church, we must put all of our effort into attaining peace — but a peace rooted in justice, a peace with dignity."

Archbishop Obeso also took up the lost thread of the Medellín conference's insistence on "structural" mechanisms of oppression, promising that the hierarchy would face up both to the serious problem of poverty in Mexico as well as the still unsatisfactory democratic transition in Mexico, by promoting "economic, social, and political models that resolve those problems [with] solutions that do not stop at good intentions, but achieve necessary structural changes." Recalling the anti-church campaign prior to the August 21 elections, Obeso told reporters that Mexico's bishops have "a very straightforward obligation to express ourselves when it is necessary" and pledged that he would try to assure that "we will not remain quiet when our voice is required."

Church sources said that Obeso's competence as an administrator, his proven ability as a negotiator, and his tolerance of progressive church sectors within his own diocese had convinced more than fifty of the seventy-four bishops who cast votes in the election that he represented the best interests of the church for the coming three years. Indeed, he was certainly a more amenable choice for progressive bishops like Samuel Ruiz and Arturo Lona, long given over to voting in CEM elections for colleagues who represented the least threat to the continuation of the pastoral programs in their own dioceses.

Three days after Obeso was chosen to lead the CEM, the Vatican announced the appointment of Archbishops Suárez Rivera and Sandoval as Mexico's two newest cardinals. For Sandoval, it was effectively a vote of confidence, given that he had run afoul of law enforcement authorities and Prigione for his insistence on the possibility that the murder of Cardinal Posadas might have been premeditated. For Suárez Rivera, it was a virtual reward for his role in the reestablishment of cordial church-state ties, while at the same time it reinforced the influence of post-Vatican II moderates within the hierarchy.

On November 1, President Salinas delivered his final state of the nation address to a joint session of Mexico's Congress, disrupted inside the congressional chambers by a PAN legislator bearing a sign that said, "Salinas, you lie." The outgoing president insisted that the events that had shaken the nation in 1994 reflected "the action of isolated individuals or groups, but they may also have been spurred by a feeling of rejection of the changes that have been made."[26] The changes, argued Salinas, were all for the good; he stressed that in 1994 his administration had increased economic growth to 3 percent of gross domestic product (GDP), while keeping inflation to just 7 percent, increasing exports to the United States by 22 percent under NAFTA and maintaining a surprisingly high level of dollar reserves, totalling more than $17 billion. What Salinas failed to mention was that the increase in Mexican exports under NAFTA was overwhelmed by the flood of imported products into the country. The combination of that trade imbalance with the fact that foreign investors, who were nervous over the country's political turmoil, increasingly had shifted their money from direct and peso-denominated investment either out of the country or into shorter-term, dollar-denominated stocks and bonds was largely responsible for an alarming current account deficit that hit $28 billion by year's end.[27]

In his quest to become Salinas's successor, Ernesto Zedillo had pledged to implement many reforms and progressive policies once in office: a political divorce of the PRI and the government, an overhaul of the country's corrupt and inefficient judicial system, and greater credit and infrastructure support for impoverished campesino subsistence farmers were just a few of his many campaign vows. In his December 1 inaugural address, Zedillo reiterated those pledges and said not only was he "convinced that it is possible to achieve in Chiapas new negotiations that will result in a just, dignified, and definitive peace," but that his administration would "break the vicious cycle of illness, ignorance, unemployment, and poverty, in which many millions of Mexicans are trapped."[28]

But Zedillo's choice of a cabinet dominated by former Salinas administration officials led many to feel that all he had to offer was six more years of the same policies. Even before taking office, Zedillo was beleaguered politically, with Mario Ruiz Massieu resigning publicly on November 28 from his post as Assistant Attorney General and charging his boss, Attorney General Benítez Treviño, with having conspired with top PRI officials to obstruct the investigation into the murder of José Francisco Ruiz Massieu. At the same time, on the economic front some analysts were expressing concerns over the rising current deficit, while business leaders showed lukewarm support for the federal budget proposal that Zedillo submitted to Congress.

But it was trouble brewing far to the south that was soon to overtake Mexico's new president. After hotly contested November 20 gubernatorial elections in Tabasco state, the local electoral commission awarded victory with 56 percent of the vote to PRI candidate Roberto Madrazo Pintado. The move sparked protests by the opposition PRD, which claimed its candidate, Manuel Andrés López Obrador, had been denied the governorship through vote fraud. As Tabasco PRD supporters staged a week-long protest in Mexico City before returning home December 6 to blockade highways and facilities of the state-oil monopoly PEMEX, a post-electoral conflict in Tabasco's neighboring state of Chiapas was also heating up.

. With the CONAI mediation team unable to arrange renewed government-rebel negotiations, Bishop Ruiz saw trouble looming. In the wake of the August 21 national elections, in which Chiapas voters also went to the polls to elect a new governor, the state electoral commission handed victory to PRI candidate Eduardo Robledo. Charges of electoral fraud were leveled by supporters of opposition PRD candidate Amado Avendaño, a lawyer and publisher of San Cristóbal's outspoken newspaper *Tiempo*. As PRD protests grew, they meshed with ongoing protests by indigenous and campesino groups over longstanding land disputes. The Zapatistas added their voice to the chorus of those demanding that Robledo not take office, warning that if he were inaugurated violence would certainly result.

On November 28, government envoy Jorge Madrazo, who had been rebuffed on the twelve separate occasions that he tried to contact the rebels directly, stepped aside to allow Zedillo to appoint a new peace commissioner. That same day, Ruiz told reporters in Guadalajara that until December 8 he still had hopes that peace could prevail. "But if at that time there is simply a decision to impose someone who has been legally declared the [gubernatorial election] winner," Ruiz said, "what will occur is...an explicable polarization." On December 1, Ruiz called for alternative proposals to those presented by Madrazo and sketched the CONAI's own bare-bones plan aimed at simply getting the two sides to the negotiating table. It was to no avail, however, as that same day Chiapas PRD leaders used the occasion of Zedillo's inauguration to announce that they would block access to the state capital of Tuxtla Gutiérrez during Robledo's December 8 inauguration and hold a parallel swearing-in ceremony for Avendaño.

Secretly, Zedillo and the Zapatistas had been exchanging letters since before December 1, and on one occasion the Zapatistas had met with Zedillo envoy Esteban Moctezuma, who was in line to became Interior Secretary in the new presidential cabinet. The parleys were fruitless, however, and on December 8 Zedillo attended Robledo's inauguration ceremony, during which Robledo promised to step down if the Zapatistas would first lay down their arms. The stage was set for a showdown, as Bishop Ruiz celebrated a Mass for peace in San Cristóbal, saying during his homily that the situation was "grave, in as much as at this moment there are two states of Chiapas, two governors, two governments and two armies. This is the beginning of civil war."[29]

But war did not break out — at least, not yet. On December 14, after a quick trip to Miami to talk up Latin American free trade at a hemispheric summit of thirty-four heads of state, Zedillo tried to bypass Bishop Ruiz's CONAI by proposing a joint legislative peace commission, comprised of members of all the parties in Congress, to mediate negotiations between the government and the rebels. The Zapatista response was not long in coming. On December 19, after eleven ominous days of silence from the jungle following Robledo's inauguration, journalists in San Cristóbal were summoned to an early morning press conference in rebel-held territory near the town of Guadalupe Tepeyac, during which the rebels' Subcommander Marcos claimed that Zapatista columns had filtered past the army back into the Chiapas highlands and were staging highway and town hall takeovers in thirty-eight municipalities statewide.

Upon hearing the news, Ruiz immediately called a press conference and pronounced himself to be on an indefinite "fast for peace" in order to pressure for resumed negotiations. In the highlands town of Simojovel, Father Joel Padrón watched as a group of masked Zapatista supporters took over the town hall and then "read statements of support for the Zapatistas over a loudspeaker, denouncing Robledo and supporting Avendaño."[30] Like others who observed the town takeovers and highway blockades, Padrón said it was not clear if they were Zapatista troops or local supporters wearing ski masks, but the actions statewide seemed "to have been very well coordinated."

In and of itself, the Zapatistas' show of force would not have had major political or economic repercussions under normal circumstances. But apparently in an attempt to lay the blame for distasteful economic policy decisions on the Zapatistas, the Zedillo administration tried to use the December 19 political turmoil as a cover for a relatively minor, yet much-needed devaluation of the Mexican peso. The current deficit had gotten way out of hand, so much so that Mexico's dollar reserves had been drained to just above $5 billion, their lowest point since 1988. Although government officials had promised no currency devaluation, in order to stem the tide of falling dollar reserves a devaluation was deemed necessary as a means of making Mexican goods more competitive, both at home and abroad, and of fueling direct foreign investment in the economy.

In an early-morning announcement on December 20, Finance Secretary

Jaime Serra announced the decision to let the peso move to the edge of its fixed exchange band against the U.S. dollar, effectively devaluing the currency by 15 percent. What followed, however, was a financial disaster for Mexico. The Mexico City stock exchange plummeted, interest rates rose by more than 50 percent and there was a major run on the peso. Late on December 21, Serra announced the peso would be allowed to float freely against the dollar and within twenty-four hours the Mexican currency had lost 30 percent of its value — and was still falling. The debacle led to Serra's forced resignation on December 29 amid shattered investor confidence in Mexico. Following an urgent visit to Mexico by a delegation of the International Monetary Fund, Zedillo was forced on January 3 to outline an economic austerity plan that included a not-very-effective ceiling on price and wage hikes, as well as cuts to federal spending.

In less than two weeks, the neoliberal economic program designed by former President Salinas and his advisors had come crashing down. Even after the massive sell-off of state-owned industries that helped pay down the foreign debt in 1990, Mexico once again was on the advent of a foreign debt crisis — with the debt denominated in dollars, the devaluation shrunk Mexico's gross domestic product (GDP) in dollar terms by more than 30 percent, thereby increasing Mexico's foreign debt from 23.5 percent of GDP prior to the devaluation to 41.3 percent of GDP at year's end.[31] Foreign governments and lending institutions rallied to the Zedillo administration's aid, promising a financial bailout package. But by late January the U.S. Congress was battling along partisan lines as to whether or not the U.S. Treasury should act as a guarantor on $40 billion worth of private loans to Mexico, with some analysts doubting whether that sum would be sufficient to stabilize the buffeted Mexican economy.

In the midst of the crisis, the necessity of stabilizing the Chiapas situation loomed large for the Zedillo administration. In a December 21 statement, the Mexican Bishops Conference called on Zedillo to end the "situation of violence" in Chiapas and expressed support for Bishop Ruiz's fast, which had since been emulated by another twenty-three individuals nationwide, including Mexican actress Ofelia Medina and Bishop Arturo Lona of Tehuantepec. On December 23, Zedillo sent Interior Undersecretary Beatriz Paredes to Chiapas to meet with CONAI members and establish contact with the Zapatistas. Five days later, the Mexican Army obeyed direct orders from Zedillo and pulled back its units from forward positions, to which the Zapatistas responded with a pledge to pull back its troops near four towns at the entrances to rebel-held territory. Because he said he had not yet seen sufficient signals from either side that they were willing to re-enter negotiations, however, Bishop Ruiz did not end his fast immediately. Following a January 1 announcement by the Zapatistas of a six-day unilateral cease fire, after sixteen days, on January 4, Ruiz broke his fast, saying during an ecumenical service in San Cristóbal's "Cathedral of Peace" that he remained uneasy about the prospects for lasting peace.

After further cease-fire extensions and military pullbacks, the CONAI established contact between the government and the Zapatistas. On January 15, Interior Secretary Moctezuma met secretly with the Zapatistas in rebel-held territory, and the next day the rebels extended their cease fire indefinitely. Two days later, President Zedillo presided over the January 17 signing in Mexico City of a national political accord in which leaders of the PRI, the PRD, the PAN and the fledgling Labor Party (PT) agreed to work toward the "immediate resolution of post-electoral conflicts" nationwide. The next day, Bishop Ruiz and the other seven CONAI members met in full assembly in Mexico City, and sources close to the commission said an important announcement was expected. But no such announcement came and Bishop Ruiz returned to Chiapas as news of post-electoral turmoil in Tabasco state intervened to cut immediate Chiapas peace hopes short.

With the dispute in Tabasco reaching the boiling point, on January 16 newly appointed Bishop Florencio Olvera had publicly declared himself neutral and called on the government to determine if there had been fraud in the November 20 elections.[32] The next day, responding to reports that Zedillo had asked Tabasco governor Madrazo Pintado to resign to facilitate a negotiated settlement, local PRI members staged a blockade of the state capital, Villahermosa. On January 18, rock-hurling and club-wielding PRIistas with the support of police and the army violently drove PRD protesters from Villahermosa's main plaza, which they had occupied since December 31 to keep Madrazo Pintado from entering state government offices. Jesuit Father Francisco Goitia, president of the independent Tabasco Human Rights Commission, charged that the ousting of the PRD "was made to look as though it was done by the [local] PRI, but the entire operation was clearly planned ahead of time by the state government."[33] Many observers agreed with Lorenzo Meyer, a political analyst at Mexico City's graduate research institute, El Colegio de México, who said the Tabasco PRI militants would not have dared the ouster "had they sensed the president was strong; . . . they must have 'smelled blood.' "[34]

Zedillo had clearly intended to press forward to resolve some of Mexico's more serious social problems in the first days of his administration. He introduced a sweeping judicial reform package into Congress and authorized Attorney General Lozano Gracia — a member of the opposition PAN — to reopen the investigations into the Posadas, Colosio, and Ruiz Massieu murders. On December 16, Lozano appointed a new special prosecutor in the cases, Pablo Chapa Benzanilla, who refused to rule out any hypotheses[35] and who later met publicly with Cardinal Sandoval in Guadalajara, accepting as evidence the testimonies rebuffed earlier by former Assistant Attorney General Mario Ruiz Massieu.[36] Likewise, in the first week of January, Interior Secretary Moctezuma showed the administration's openness in meeting with a number of Catholic priests known for their work with the poor, which one priest said reflected a government willingness to "establish a dialogue" as to how best to alleviate the suffering of Mexico's marginalized classes.[37]

But whether Zedillo would be able to deal effectively with the serious social, political, and economic problems confronting his administration remained to be seen. As a result of inflation, the purchasing power of minimum-wage-earning workers had fallen 7 percent since 1994 and 26.6 percent since 1988.[38] Because of the peso devaluation and rise in interest rates, some analysts expected inflation to resurge and top 20 percent in 1995. With the country's automotive industry ground to a near halt, the construction industry in crisis, and layoffs reported throughout the private sector, rising unemployment threatened to become a major problem.

Meanwhile, the undercapitalized banking sector, which had been threatening to foreclose on loans to farmers for months, began to put the squeeze on urban homeowners and consumers whose payments on mortgages and credit cards were past due. In the countryside, campesino subsistence farmer organizations were upset because fixed price levels for basic grains under the new austerity plan were inadequate, while PROCAMPO subsidies were cut to levels far below what was previously agreed.[39]

U.S. Congressional demands that Mexico's oil be used as collateral for the loan guarantee package or that illegal immigration to the United States and Mexico's diplomatic support for Cuba become riders to the bailout package were publicly rejected by the Mexican president.[40] But their very inclusion in the debate complicated Zedillo's room for political maneuver, as did the fact that any loan package certainly would be tied to further austerity measures. A promised increase in privatization of the state-owned telecommunications and railroad industries pointed to the possibility that Mexico's state-owned petroleum industry might also be privatized. And with more cuts to federal spending a certainty, some observers believed that one victim would be Solidarity, the controversial Salinista social-welfare program that Zedillo had pledged to maintain.

As the Mexican government faced a crisis situation, no less critical was the situation facing the Mexican church. Within the church, there were the questions of the key appointment of a new archbishop of Mexico City, sure to succeed Ernesto Corripio as cardinal. There was also the appointment of four new bishops to the as-yet-to-be-defined Mexico City metropolitan dioceses, giving the current Vatican administration and Archbishop Prigione say in the naming of another four Mexican bishops. But more important was the church's pastoral response to the country's problems. Bishop Ruiz continued his controversial quest for peace in Chiapas, while the Mexican church hierarchy was called on to issue pastoral guidance on the economic crisis and electoral disputes in Chiapas, Tabasco, Veracruz, and other states. Individual bishops called for unity in the face of the crisis, apparently afraid that frustration over continued economic austerity might spark greater political upheaval. Archbishop Obeso warned reporters on January 23 that the country ran the risk of turning local electoral problems into violent national conflicts. Criticizing the PRI's ouster of the PRD in Tabasco, Obeso cautioned that "the dangerous thing about these new mobilizations is in the way they attempt to quash a situation with violent actions that are in nobody's interest."[41]

As Mexican society lurched forward into this new crisis, the questions of how the church should respond to flawed democracy, to human rights abuse, and to socio-economic inequities continued to divide the hierarchy and the bases — lay Catholics, religious, and the "lower clergy" — at least in practice, if not so much in principle. Throughout history, the Mexican Catholic Church's reaction to similar questions has been mixed: at times it has sided with the powerful; at times it has defended and taken up the cause of the poor. At times it has straddled the fence and ended up caught in the turmoil it was unable to prevent.

Sometimes magnificently, sometimes in imperfect measure, the Mexican church will continue to respond to such issues. In a country where nearly half the population continues to languish in poverty, while the wealthy enrich themselves largely unhindered at the expense of the majority, there are those who understand the need to confront the issues by speaking out decisively. On the day of his election to a third term as president of the CEM, Archbishop Obeso told the press that denouncing social injustice "is simply [a matter of] following the Gospel, which tells us that a prophet must speak out. If his words have negative consequences for himself or for his group, then he just has to face up to it." Archbishop Obeso's words could not have been more timely. As Mexico entered what promised to be a tumultuous 1995, it was clear that the laity, religious, and hierarchy of the Mexican Catholic Church were pulling up to another crossroads in their history. The question was whether they would speak out clearly or their voices would remain muffled or even silent. The answer was one that only time could tell.

Notes

Chapter 1: Rebellion in the Promised Land

1. Matilde Pérez and Rosa Rojas, "Comandante Marcos: El EZLN tiene 10 años de preparación," *La Jornada* (Mexico City), January 2, 1994, 4.

2. *Estadísticas históricas de México*, vol. 1 (Mexico City: Instituto Nacional de Estadística, Geografía e Informática, 1985).

3. Anna María Garza Caligaris and María Fernanda Paz Salinas, "Las migraciones: Testimonios de una historia viva," *Anuario CEI* (San Cristóbal de las Casas: Centro de Estudios Indígenas, Universidad Autónoma de Chiapas, 1986), 1:95.

4. Samuel Ruiz, interview with author, San Cristóbal, October 7, 1991.

5. Mario Humberto Ruz S., "Los Tojolobales," in Victor Manuel Esponda, comp., *La población indígena de Chiapas* (Tuxtla Gutiérrez, Mexico: Instituto Chiapaneco de Cultura, 1993), 292.

6. Garza Caligaris and Paz Salinas, "Las migraciones," 91.

7. Eugenio Maurer, interview with author, Mexico City, June 9, 1994.

8. Samuel Ruiz García, "In This Hour of Grace," *Origins* (CNS Documentary Service, Washington, D.C.) 23, no. 34 (February 10, 1994): 597–98.

9. Ibid., 598.

10. Ibid.

11. Ibid.

12. Eugenio Maurer, interview with author, Mexico City, June 9, 1994.

13. Pablo Iribarren Pascal, *Los dominicos en la pastoral indígena* (Mexico City: Formación Permanente, 1991), 11.

14. Pablo Iribarren, "La inculturación de la Iglesia en la praxis de la comunidad tzeltal," *Amanesis* (Mexico City), no. 1 (January–June 1991): 147.

15. Pablo Iribarren, "Del ministerio del Tuhunel," unpublished ms., n.d., Mexico City, 2.

16. Iribarren, *Los dominicos*, 51; Samuel Ruiz, interview with author, San Cristóbal, June 2, 1994.

17. Neil Harvey, *Rebellion in Chiapas: Rural Reforms, Campesino Radicalism, and the Limits to Salinismo* (San Diego, Calif.: Center for U.S.-Mexican Studies, University of California at San Diego, 1994), 28.

18. Iribarren, *Los dominicos*, 51.

19. Ignacio Ramírez, "Grupos de izquierda de Torreón utilizaron la infraestructura religiosa y radicalizaron a los catequistas: Samuel Ruiz," *Proceso* (Mexico City), no. 904 (February 28, 1994): 9.

20. Francisco Ornelas, "Por si se aclara lo de Chiapas: Resumen de muchas presentaciones," *Noticias de la Provincia*, Society of Jesus, Mexico City (April–May 1994): 10; Pablo Iribarren, interview with author, Puebla, Mexico, June 16, 1994.

21. Neil Harvey, *Rebellion in Chiapas*, 23.

22. Ibid.

23. "Comunicado de prensa," Diocese of San Cristóbal de las Casas, August 2, 1990.

24. Joel Padrón, interview with author, Cerro Hueco penitentiary, Tuxtla Gutiérrez, Mexico, October 7, 1991.

25. Ann Louise Bardach, "Mexico's Poet Rebel," *Vanity Fair* (July 1994): 131.

26. José Antonio Román, "La carta que entregué al papa, causa del encono: Samuel Ruiz," *La Jornada* (Mexico City), December 16, 1993, 15.

27. Ruiz García, "In This Hour," 600.

28. Jesús Vergara Aceves and Leonardo Méndez, "¿Un México nuevo?: Análisis de la realidad nacional, año de 1993" (Mexico City: Centro Tata Vasco, 1994), 90–100.

29. Canadian Catholic Organization for Development and Peace, "Press Communiqué: Canadian Delegation to Chiapas," Montreal, January 1994; Americas Watch, "The New Year's Rebellion: Violations of Human Rights and Humanitarian Law during the Armed Revolt in Chiapas, Mexico," *Americas Watch Report* 6, no. 3 (March 1, 1994); Amnesty International, "Amnesty International's Research Mission to Chiapas (January 15–26, 1994)," London, 1994.

Chapter 2: From Conquest to Revolution

1. Clodomiro L. Siller Acuña, *Para comprender el mensaje de María de Guadalupe* (Buenos Aires: Editorial Guadalupe, 1989), 60.

2. Ibid., 25, 69–70.

3. Robert Ricard, *La conquista espiritual de México* (Mexico City: Fondo de Cultura Económica, 1986), 98–100.

4. Ernest Gruening, *Mexico and Its Heritage* (New York: Century Co., 1928), 115.

5. Alejandra Moreno Toscana, "El siglo de la conquista," in *Historia general de México*, vol. 1 (Mexico City: SEP/El Colegio de México, 1981), 56.

6. Agustín Yáñez, *Fray Bartolomé de las Casas: El conquistador conquistado* (Mexico City: Editorial Xochitl, 1949), 149–51.

7. Ricard, *La conquista*, 131.

8. Stafford Poole, "The Third Mexican Provincial Council of 1585 and the Reform of the Diocesan Clergy," in Jeffrey A. Cole, ed., *The Church and Society in Latin America* (New Orleans: Center for Latin American Studies, Tulane University, 1984), 22–23; John Frederick Schwaller, "The Implementation of the Ordenanza de Patronazgo in New Spain," in ibid., 40.

9. Moisés González Navarro, *Repartimiento de indios en Nueva Galicia* (Mexico City: INAH, 1953), 11–12.

10. Enrique Florescano and Isabel Gil Sánchez, "La época de las reformas borbónicas y el crecimiento económico," *Historia general de México*, vol. 2, 196.

11. Howard F. Cline, *The United States and Mexico* (New York: Atheneum, 1963), 34.

12. Gruening, *Mexico and Its Heritage*, 178–79.

13. Guillermo Bonfil Batalla, *México profundo* (Mexico City: Grijalbo, 1990), 147.

14. Jacques Gabayet Jacqueton, "El milenarismo radical y la hermeneútica de las clases poderosas en México," in Martín de la Rosa and Charles A. Reilly, *Religión y política en México* (Mexico City: Siglo XXI/University of California at San Diego, Center for U.S.-Mexican Studies, 1985), 83.

15. Ibid., 85.

16. Ibid., 81.

17. Rodolfo Casillas, "La discusión sobre el patronato eclesiástico," in María Alicia Puente Lutteroth, comp., *Hacia una historia mínima de la Iglesia en México* (Mexico City: Editorial JUS/CEHILA, 1993), 94; José Miguel Romero de Solís, *El aguijón del espíritu: Historia contemporánea de la Iglesia en México (1895–1990)* (Mexico City: Instituto Mexicano de Doctrina Social, 1994), 51.

18. Samuel Trujillo González, "Nuevos grupos religiosos en Mexico (1930–1989)," in Puente Lutteroth, comp., *Hacia una historia mínima*, 199.

19. Jean-Pierre Bastian, *Los disidentes: Sociedades protestantes y revolución en México, 1872–1911* (Mexico City: Fondo de Cultura Económica, 1989), 87–90; also Jean-Pierre Bastian, "Disidencia religiosa en el campo mexicano," in De la Rosa and Reilly, *Religión y política*, 179; and Rubén Ruiz Guera, "Historia del protestantismo 1870–1930," in Puente Lutteroth, *Hacia una historia*, 122–24.

20. Romero de Solís, *El aguijón*, 51.

21. Puente Lutteroth, "Repercusiones sociales de una política de conciliación: Iglesia y Porfiriato (1876–1910)," *Hacia una historia*, 130–31.

22. Romero de Solís, *El aguijón*, 34.

23. Ibid., 30.

24. Ibid., 31.

25. Bastian, *Los disidentes*, 312.

26. Romero de Solís, *El aguijón*, 53.

27. Jean Meyer, *El catolicismo social en México hasta 1913* (Mexico City: Instituto Mexicano de Doctrina Social Cristiana, 1985), 11, 13.

28. Jean Meyer, *La Cristiada*, vol. 2: *El conflicto entre la Iglesia y el Estado* (Mexico City: Siglo XXI, 1980), 102.

29. Romero de Solís, *El aguijón*, 112.

30. Meyer, *El catolicismo social*, 20.

31. Romero de Solís, *El aguijón*, 162.

32. Meyer, *La Cristiada*, vol. 2, 64.

33. Gruening, *Mexico and Its Heritage*, 136.

34. Gabayet Jacqueton, "El milenarismo radical," 89–90; María Alicia Puente de Guzmán, "Revolución mexicana," in Puente Lutteroth, comp., *Hacia una historia*, 149; Meyer, *La Cristiada*, vol. 2, 95–96.

35. Bastian, *Los disidentes*, 290.

36. Meyer, *La Cristiada*, vol. 2, 96.

37. Ibid, 96; John Womack, Jr., *Zapata and the Mexican Revolution* (New York: Vintage, 1970), 162.

38. Romero de Solís, *El aguijón*, 191, 251.

39. Meyer, *La Cristiada*, vol. 2, 102.

40. Ibid., 97–99.

41. Ibid., 97, 99.

42. Romero de Solís, *El aguijón*, 201–3.

Chapter 3: From Cristo Rey to Tlatelolco

1. José Miguel Romero de Solís, *El aguijón del espíritu: Historia contemporánea de la Iglesia en México (1895–1990)* (Mexico City: Instituto Mexicano de Doctrina Social, 1994), 255.

2. Dan La Botz, "Roberto Haberman and the Origins of Modern Mexico's Jewish Community," *American Jewish Archives* 153, no. 1 (Spring/Summer 1991): 15–18.

3. Jean-Pierre Bastian, *Los disidentes: Sociedades protestantes y revolución en México, 1872–1911* (Mexico City: Fondo de Cultura Económica, 1989), 271–92.

4. Ibid., 292–93; Jean Meyer, *La Cristiada*, vol. 2: *El conflicto entre la Iglesia y el Estado* (Mexico City: Siglo XXI, 1980), 195–96.

5. Samuel Ramos, *Profile of Man and Culture in Mexico* (Austin: University of Texas Press, 1975), 169.

6. Ibid., 169.

7. Ernest Gruening, *Mexico and Its Heritage* (New York: Century Co., 1928), 525.

8. Andrés Molina Enríquez, quoted in Bonfil Batalla, *México profundo*, 164.

9. Guillermo Bonfil Batalla, *México profundo* (Mexico City: Grijalbo, 1990), 42.

10. Philip Russell, *Mexico in Transition* (Austin, Tex.: Colorado River Press, 1977), 40.

11. Meyer, *La Cristiada*, vol. 1: *La guerra de los cristeros* (Mexico City: Siglo XXI, 1980), 31, 49.

12. Lorenzo Meyer, "El primer tramo del camino," in *Historia general de México*, 135; Jean Meyer, *La Cristiada*, vol. 3: *Los Cristeros* (Mexico City: Siglo XXI, 1980), 77–78; Gruening, *Mexico and Its Heritage*, 152–53.

13. Meyer, *La Cristiada*, vol. 3, 294.

14. Meyer, *La Cristiada*, vol. 1, 182, 191, 208–10, 218–19, 255–56, 269.

15. Romero de Solís, *El aguijón*, 308; Meyer, *La Cristiada*, vol. 1, 315.

16. Servando Otoll, "Faccionarismo episcopal en México y la revolución cristera," in De la Rosa and Reilly, *Religión y política*, 30–39.

17. Roberto Blancarte, *Historia de la Iglesia católica en México, 1929–1982* (Mexico City: Fondo de Cultura Económica, 1992), 29.

18. Meyer, *La Cristiada*, vol. 1, 375.

19. David Stoll, *Fishers of Men or Founders of Empire?* (London: Zed Press, 1982), 62–75.

20. Blancarte, *Historia de la Iglesia*, 105.

21. Romero de Solís, *El aguijón*, 410.

22. "Carta pastoral del excmo. y rvmo. Sr. Arzobispo de México sobre la cruzada en defensa de nuestra fe," *Christus* 10, no. 110 (January 1945): 10.

23. Bonfil Batalla, *México profundo*, 178–79.

24. Jean-Pierre Bastian, "Disidencia religiosa protestante y imperialismo en México," in Miguel Concha et al., *La participación de los cristianos en el proceso popular de liberación en México* (Mexico City: Instituto de Investigaciones Sociales, UNAM/Siglo XXI, 1986), 296.

25. Ibid., 297–98.

26. Ibid., 295.

27. Ibid., 183.

28. Romero de Solís, *El aguijón*, 51, 413.

29. Russell, *Mexico in Transition*, 90.

30. Ibid.

31. Soledad Loaeza, "Notas para el estudio de la Iglesia en el México contemporáneo," in De la Rosa and Reilly, *Religión y política*, 49.

32. Romero de Solís, *El aguijón*, 411, 413, 415.

33. Alejandro Gálvez, "La Iglesia y el gobierno de López Mateos," in De la Rosa and Reilly, *Religión y política*, 65.

34. Gabriela Videla, *Sergio Méndez Arceo: Un señor obispo* (Mexico City: Editorial Nuevomar, 1984), 41–42.

35. Ibid., 39.

36. Jesús García, "La Iglesia en México desde la creación del CELAM hasta Puebla," in Puente Lutteroth, *Hacia una historia mínima,* 185.

37. Blancarte, *Historia de la Iglesia,* 233.

38. Ibid., 232, 236.

Chapter 4: Medellín and the Vatican's Silent Offensive

1. Miguel Concha et al., *La participación de los cristianos en el proceso popular de liberación en México* (Mexico City: Instituto de Investigaciones Sociales, UNAM/Siglo XXI, 1986), 89–90; Roberto Blancarte, *Historia de la Iglesia católica en México, 1929–1982* (Mexico City: Fondo de Cultura Económica, 1992), 243.

2. Enrique Maza, "El movimiento estudiantil y sus repercusiones," *Christus,* no. 397 (December 1968): 1263.

3. "Mensaje pastoral sobre el movimiento estudiantil," October 9, 1968, *Documentos colectivos del episcopado Mexicano 1965–1975* (Mexico City: Ediciones Paulinas, 1976), 117–21.

4. Concha et al., *La participación de los cristianos,* 79.

5. José Miguel Romero de Solís, *El aguijón del espíritu: Historia contemporánea de la Iglesia en México (1895–1990)* (Mexico City: Instituto Mexicano de Doctrina Social, 1994), 454–55.

6. Blancarte, *Historia de la Iglesia,* 249.

7. Ibid., 266.

8. Juan Guerra (amnestied member of Liga 23 affiliate group Los Enfermos and federal congressman), interview with author, August 13, 1994, Mexico City.

9. *Fundamentos teológicos de la pastoral indígena en México* (Mexico City: Comisión Episcopal para Indígenas, CEM, 1988).

10. Bartolomé Carrasco, "Aprehensiones en Tapachula: Mensaje de reflexión," *Documentación e Información Católica* (DIC) 2, no. 18 (May 2, 1974): 188; Arturo Lona, "Injusticias en el Istmo de Tehuantepec: Revelan obispos y sacerdotes," *DIC* 4, no. 21 (May 20, 1976): 206; Samuel Ruiz, "Situaciones de injusticia y violencia en Chiapas," *DIC* 4, no. 22 (May 27, 1976): 219.

11. Blancarte, *Historia de la Iglesia católica,* 308–11.

12. Concha et al., *La participación de los cristianos,* 159.

13. Ibid., 153–56.

14. Ignacio Ramírez, "Grupos de izquierda de Torreón utilizaron la infraestructura religiosa y radicalizaron a los catequistas: Samuel Ruiz," *Proceso* (Mexico City), no. 904 (February 28, 1994): 9; Carlos Marín "La guerrilla aprovechó la estructura de las comunidades cristianas," *Síntesis* (Puebla, Mexico), January 3, 1994, 14.

15. *El magisterio pastoral de la región Pacífico Sur,* vol. 3: *Tehuantepec 1891–1991: Un siglo de fe* (Mexico City: CENAMI, 1991), 55–94.

16. Arturo Lona, "Decreto de excomunión a torturadores," *DIC* 9, no. 25 (June 18, 1981): 417; Sergio Méndez Arceo, "Decreto de excomunión para los torturadores en el Estado de Morelos, Diócesis de Cuernavaca," *DIC* 9, nos. 18–19 (April 30–May 7, 1981): 308.

17. "Exhortación pastoral" (Bishops of the Gulf Pastoral Region), DIC 7, no. 18 (May 3, 1979): 292.

18. "Votar con responsabilidad: Una orientación cristiana del arzobispo de Chihuahua, 15-V-83," La Iglesia habla: Orientaciones pastorales de los obispos de México sobre el tema cívico-político (1981–1987) (Monterrey: USEM, 1988), 160.

19. "Coherencia cristiana en la política: Exhortación pastoral de los obispos de la Región Norte, 19-III-86," La Iglesia habla, 203.

20. Concha et al., La participación de los cristianos, 168–69.

21. Margaret Hooks, "Mexico's Bishop Lona Stands with Indian Groups in Struggle for Rights," Latinamerica Press, October 3, 1985, 6.

22. Blancarte, Historia de la Iglesia, 271.

23. Romero de Solís, El aguijón, 415.

24. Noelle Montiel, "Las mujeres, instrumento de la Iglesia institucional para mantener las estructuras de dominación," in De la Rosa and Reilly, Religión y política, 158.

25. Gabriela Videla, Sergio Méndez Arceo: Un señor obispo (Mexico City: Editorial Nuevomar, 1984), 85–86.

26. Rogelio Sánchez et al., Expresión eclesial: Realidad de las pequeñas comunidades cristianas en México (Mexico City: Palmarín, 1971), 12; Concha et al., La participación de los cristianos, 233.

27. Sergio Méndez Arceo, "Comentario dominical breve de la dedicación de la nueva basílica," DIC 4, no. 44 (October 28, 1976): 533.

28. Concha et al., La participación de los cristianos, 96, 149– 50; Blancarte, Historia de la Iglesia, 326–27.

29. Romero de Solís, El aguijón, 456–58.

30. José Alvarez Icaza, "El primer viaje del papa a México," unpublished ms., Mexico City, 1990, 1.

31. John Eagleson and Philip Scharper, eds., Puebla and Beyond (Maryknoll, N.Y.: Orbis Books, 1979), 142.

32. Concha et al., La participación de los cristianos, 114.

33. Emilio Hernández, "Echeverría impuso a José López Portillo su Plan de Alianza con la Iglesia," Proceso (Mexico City), no. 447 (May 27, 1985): 6–11.

34. Blancarte, Historia de la Iglesia, 402.

35. Concha et al., La participación de los cristianos, 84.

36. Homero Campa and Rodrigo Vera, "Los colegios religiosos, trampolín al poder público," Proceso (Mexico City), no. 559 (July 20, 1987): 6–10.

37. Rodrigo Vera, "La jerarquía, en combate contra seguidores de Méndez Arceo y su obra en Morelos," Proceso (Mexico City), no. 648 (April 3, 1989): 16–19.

38. "Narcotráfico, preocupación pastoral," El magisterio pastoral, 255–90.

39. M. Tangeman, "Mexican Bishops Fear Issuing Pastoral Letter," CNS cable, The Tidings (Los Angeles), May 15, 1987, 10.

40. Jaime Pérez Mendoza, "Por petición de Bartlett el Vaticano ordenó que hubiera misas en Chihuahua," Proceso (Mexico City), no. 509 (August 4, 1986): 6–17.

41. M. Tangeman, "Evangelization 2000 and Lumen 2000: Their Impacts on the Catholic Faith in the Developing World," paper presented at conference on "Faith and Development: Oppressive Christianity in the Third World," Regents College, London, October 1989.

42. M. Tangeman, "Mexican Bishop Says Previous Governments Worsened Debt Problems," CNS cable, January 29, 1987.

43. M. Tangeman, "Mexican Church Official Says Bishops Have Preference among Candidates," CNS cable, August 14, 1987.

Chapter 5: Salinismo, the Church and Quid Pro Quo

1. Sergio Obeso Rivera, "Mensaje de apertura," November 14, 1988, Fifty-third Plenary Assembly of the Mexican Bishops Conference, DIC 16, no. 48 (December 1, 1988): 939.
2. Tracy Early, "Mexican Bishops OK Plan to Expand 'Debt for Equity' Swap," CNS cable, November 2, 1988.
3. Luis Reynoso Cervantes, "Aspectos éticos de la autoridad política y de la participación política," DIC 16, no. 30 (July 28, 1988): 554–57.
4. "Conferencia del episcopado mexicano: Declaración de los obispos sobre el proceso electoral," DIC 16, no. 36 (September 8, 1988): 663–65.
5. Obeso Rivera, "Mensaje de apertura," DIC 16, no. 48 (December 1, 1988): 939.
6. "Obispos de México en visita 'Ad Limina Apostolorum,'" DIC 16, no. 43 (October 27, 1988): 815–19.
7. "Obispos mexicanos piden donativos en Washington para intercambiarlos por deuda externa," Proceso (Mexico City), no. 691 (January 29, 1990): 12–15.
8. Obeso Rivera, "Mensaje de apertura," DIC 16, no. 48 (December 1, 1988): 939.
9. M. Tangeman, "Mexican Bishops to Monitor Rights Abuses," CNS cable, Texas Catholic (Dallas), August 17, 1990, 11.
10. Hector González M. and Arnulfo Hernández, "VII Encuentro Nacional de promotores de pastoral social, derechos humanos y Caritas: Conclusiones," September 1992, typescript.
11. Laurie Hansen, "Mexican Bishops Say Restructuring Debt Not Enough to End Crisis," CNS cable, January 29, 1990.
12. M. Tangeman, "Mexico Said to Seek Vatican Emissary Letter on Clergy Visas," CNS cable, December 17, 1990; also "Papal Delegate Endorses Clergy Visa Bids, Mexican Bishops Say," CNS cable, July 30, 1991; correspondence, Secretaría de Gobernación, oficio nos. 72106 (re: Ernesto Secundino Gutiérrez Carrión), 72107 (re: Miguel Obando y Bravo, Arturo Rivera Damas, Rodolfo Quezada Toruño), 72598 (re: Jorge Mario Avila), 72725 (re: Edy Montenegro, Miguel Ovando [sic] Bravo); correspondence, Apostolic Delegation in Mexico, November 8, 1990 (to Lic. Susana Torres Hernández, director of Mexican Immigration Services); correspondence, Ecuadoran Bishops' Conference, oficio nos. 1271/90, 1272/90, 1273/90.
13. Marcos Chávez M. and Luis Acevedo Pesquera, "A la marginación social, 15 millones de mexicanos," El Financiero (Mexico City), September 26, 1994, 38.
14. Carlos Fernández-Vega, "La elite del empresariado mexicano," Perfil de la Jornada, April 1, 1991, I.
15. José Luis Calva, "La política social," El Financiero (Mexico City), September 15, 1994, 32.
16. Ibid.
17. Claudia Fernández, "Mexican Billionaires Booming," El Financiero International Edition, July 11–17, 1994, 3.
18. Genaro Alamilla Arteaga, telephone interview with author, September 5, 1991.
19. Manuel Robles, "Fondos de Pronasol para remodelar y construir templos y hasta

casas para sacerdotes," *Proceso* (Mexico City), no. 761 (June 3, 1991): 12–17; Sergio Obeso, "Carta del Arzobispo Obeso," *Proceso* (Mexico City), no. 764 (June 24, 1991): 64.

20. Ignacio Uribe Najera, "Vasta con tener ojos para observar: Prigione," *La Jornada* (Mexico City), August 11, 1991, 9.

21. "Una Experiencia de SWAP-SOCIAL en Mexico," *Cuadernos de Divulgación y Análisis* 2 (Mexico City: FAPRODE/FAC, n.d.), 13–14.

22. John Paul II, homily, Chalco, May 7, 1990, Vatican press release no. 3, 3.

23. "Durango, el papa ante los empresarios: 'La actitud de servicio debe caracterizar vuestro quehacer," press bulletin no. 21, Vatican Press Office, May 9, 1990, 1.

24. "El papa en México," CENCOS press release, May 8, 1990, 1.

25. "Carta de laicos mexicanos a Juan Pablo II," April 15, 1990, typescript; "La visita del papa podría ser manipulada: Sacerdotes," *La Jornada* (Mexico City), April 16, 1990, 7, 8.

26. "Homilia para el Oficio de Vísperas de Mons. Juan Sandoval Iñiguez," *DIC* 18, no. 30 (July 16, 1990): 703.

27. Mark Pattison, "Trade Representative, Bishop Push for Open Trade with Mexico," CNS cable, May 23, 1991.

28. "Consulta de la presidencia de la Conferencia Episcopal de Estados Unidos de América sobre el Tratado de Libre Comercio con México: Consideraciones," CEM, Mexico City, May 18, 1991, typescript.

29. "USCC Official Says U.S.-Mexico Trade Accord Can Be Beneficial," CNS cable, June 11, 1991.

30. Carlos Salinas de Gortari, *Political Participation, Public Investment, and Support for the System: A Comparative Study of Rural Communities in Mexico* (San Diego, Calif.: Center for U.S.-Mexican Studies, University of California at San Diego, 1982).

31. Adolfo Suárez Rivera, telephone interview with author, August 19, 1991.

32. Carlos Salinas de Gortari, "Tercer informe de gobierno," *La Jornada* (Mexico City), November 2, 1991, XIII.

33. Neil Harvey, *Rebellion in Chiapas: Rural Reforms, Campesino Radicalism, and the Limits to Salinismo* (San Diego, Calif.: Center for U.S.-Mexican Studies, University of California at San Diego, 1994), 27.

34. Rosalba Carrasco Licea and Francisco Hernández y Puente, "La pobreza rural, problema crítico," *La Jornada* (Mexico City), April 16, 1994, 55.

35. M. Tangeman, "Mexican Bishops Want to Put Evangelization Record Right," CNS cable, October 4, 1990.

36. Bartolomé Carrasco, Arturo Lona, Hermenegildo Ramírez, and Samuel Ruiz, "Santo Domingo y la pastoral indígena," April 1993.

37. Samuel Ruiz García, "In This Hour of Grace," *Origins* (CNS Documentary Service, Washington, D.C.) 23, no. 34 (February 10, 1994): 592.

38. "Imputaciones," apostolic delegation in Mexico, Mexico City, 1993, typescript.

Chapter 6: Uprising, Uncertainty, Assassination

1. Luis Reynoso, telephone interview with author, October 17, 1993.

2. Carlos Quintero Arce, telephone interview with author, October 18, 1993.

3. Oscar Camacho Guzmán, "'Declaración de guerra' del Ejército Zapatista en Chiapas," *La Jornada* (Mexico City), January 2, 1994, 8.

4. Ibid.

5. L. Hernández and R. Victorio, "Toma el EZLN 4 poblados en Chiapas; Cordura, pide la SG," *Excélsior* (Mexico City), January 2, 1994, 39.

6. Neil Harvey, *Rebellion in Chiapas: Rural Reforms, Campesino Radicalism, and the Limits to Salinismo* (San Diego, Calif.: Center for U.S.-Mexican Studies, University of California at San Diego, 1994), 13.

7. Ibid., 15.

8. Pablo Iribarren, telephone interview with author, January 3, 1994.

9. Canadian Catholic Organization for Development and Peace, "Press Communiqué: Canadian Delegation to Chiapas," Montreal, January 1994, 2–3; Americas Watch, "The New Year's Rebellion: Violations of Human Rights and Humanitarian Law during the Armed Revolt in Chiapas, Mexico," *Americas Watch Report* 6, no. 3 (March 1, 1994): 16–17; Amnesty International, "Amnesty International's Research Mission to Chiapas (January 15–26, 1994)," London, 1994, 5.

10. "Involucra el gobierno chiapaneco a curas católicos," *La Jornada* (Mexico City), January 2, 1994, 6.

11. Pablo Romo, interview with author, Mexico City, January 4, 1994; Miguel Concha, interview with author, Mexico City, January 4, 1994.

12. "Los obispos de Chiapas ofrecen mediar para que cese la violencia," *El Nacional* (Mexico City), January 2, 1994, 3; José Antonio Román, "Al iniciar el conflicto se pidió a Corripio declarar contra el EZLN," *La Jornada* (Mexico City), January 14, 1994, 16.

13. José Antonio Román, "Los tres obispos de Chiapas reprueban el levantamiento," *La Jornada* (Mexico City), January 2, 1994, 9.

14. "Comunicado de las Secretarías de Gobernación, Defensa Nacional, Desarrollo Social y la Procuraduría General de la República," *La Jornada* (Mexico City), January 6, 1994, 36.

15. Salvador Guerrero Chipres, "Mesa de atención especial para Chiapas, anuncia gobernación," *La Jornada* (Mexico City), January 4, 1994, 13.

16. "Comunicado de las Secretarías," 36.

17. José Antonio Román and Oscar Camacho, "Condenan obispos de Chiapas la manipulación de indígenas," *La Jornada* (Mexico City), January 4, 1994, 21.

18. Rosa Rojas, Blanche Petrich, and Gaspar Morquechua, "Duda Samuel Ruiz que hayan 'engañado' a los indígenas," *La Jornada* (Mexico City), January 8, 1994, 7.

19. Rosa Rojas, Matilde Pérez, and Amado Avendaño, "Intenso combate en Rancho Nuevo; al menos 18 muertos y 10 heridos," *La Jornada* (Mexico City), January 3, 1994, 7.

20. José Antonio Román, "Evitar la represión, demanda el episcopado mexicano al gobierno," *La Jornada* (Mexico City), January 5, 1994, 18.

21. Victor Chávez et al., "Pide Salinas a la Iglesia católica interceder en Chiapas," *El Financiero* (Mexico City), January 5, 1994, 38.

22. José Ureña, "Clase política," *La Jornada* (Mexico City), January 16, 1994, 4.

23. Salvador Guerrero Chipres, "El EZLN ha sido apoyado por ideólogos y religiosos," *La Jornada* (Mexico City), January 8, 1994, 21.

24. Ignacio Rodríguez Reyna, "La 'Corte Imperial' bajo el fuego del ejército," *El Financiero* (Mexico City), September 28, 1994, 52–53.

25. Manuel Robles and Rodrigo Vera, "Prigione, acusado de entorpecer la paz en Chiapas y de desplazar a los jesuitas en la Tarahumara," *Proceso* (Mexico City), no. 899 (January 24, 1994): 35.

26. "Conferencia del Episcopado Mexicano: Primera visita a San Cristóbal de la Comisión Episcopal para la Paz en Chiapas" (Mexico City: CEM, 1994).

27. "¿Nos van a perdonar de no morirnos de hambre?: Marcos," *El Financiero* (Mexico City), January 21, 1994, 39.

28. Oscar Hinojosa, "Camacho y Ruiz, dispuestos a reunirse con el EZLN," *El Financiero* (Mexico City), January 23, 1994, 13.

29. Ciro Gómez Leyva, "El compromiso para la paz," *El Financiero* (Mexico City), March 2, 1994, 45–47.

30. Luis Donaldo Colosio (March 6, 1994), "Planteamiento de Donaldo Colosio: Independencia del PRI con el gobierno," *Perfil de la Jornada* (Mexico City), March 15, 1994), II.

31. "Reserves Up in First Quarter," *Mexico Insight* (July 10, 1994): 16.

32. "Declina Camacho postular su candidatura a la presidencia," *El Financiero* (Mexico City), March 23, 1994, 44.

Chapter 7: Elections and Choices: Church, Society, and the Future

1. Carlos Quintero Arce, telephone interview with author, March 23, 1994.

2. Adolfo Suárez Rivera, telephone interview with author, March 23, 1994.

3. Gabriela Coutiño, "No crear hipótesis irresponsables sobre el asesinato de Colosio, pide Samuel Ruiz," *El Financiero* (Mexico City), March 25, 1994, 64.

4. Adolfo Suárez Rivera, conversation with author, Mexico City, August 20, 1994.

5. Conferencia del Episcopado Mexicano, "Los valores para la democracia," *DIC* 22, no. 9 (March 3, 1994): 75, 77.

6. Conferencia del Episcopado Mexicano, "Por la justicia, la reconciliación y la paz en México," *DIC* 22, no. 16 (April 21, 1994): 135–36.

7. José Ureña, "Clase política," *La Jornada* (Mexico City), April 24, 1994, 4.

8. Sanjuana Martínez, "La voz de la grabadora desmiente a Samuel Ruiz y delata a su secretario Miguel Alvarez," *Proceso* (Mexico City), no. 916 (May 23, 1994): 20–25.

9. Alejandro Caballero, "EZLN: Repite el PRD vicios Priistas," *La Jornada* (Mexico City), May 17, 1994, 1.

10. EZLN, "Segunda declaración de la selva lacandona," *La Jornada* (Mexico City), June 12, 1994, 7.

11. Jesús Morales Orozco, press conference, Mexico City, July 8, 1994.

12. Rogelio Gómez Hermosillo, interview with author, Mexico City, August 18, 1994.

13. María Eugenia Mondragón and Pablo Ruiz Meza, "La entrevista de Prigione con los Arellano Félix, asunto de la SRE: Ruiz Massieu," *El Financiero* (Mexico City), August 5, 1994, 34.

14. Rafael Medina Cruz, "Ellos no fueron: La esposa de Benjamín," *Excélsior*, Mexico City (July 26, 1994): 29-A.

15. Jerónimo (Girolamo) Prigione, "Aclaración," July 27, 1994.

16. Renato Dávalos, "Plan de violencia en 12 estados; Incluye curas y guerrilla," *Excélsior*, Mexico City (July 28, 1994): 1.

17. Conferencia del Episcopado Mexicano, "Es la hora de una profunda reconciliación en México," Mexico City, August 3, 1994.

18. Salvador Corro and Julio César López, "La CND preparará la insurgencia civil ante un fraude electoral; Los radicales son minoría: Alvarez Icaza," *Proceso* (Mexico City), no. 927 (August 8, 1994): 10–13.

19. Alianza Cívica/Observación 94, "Las elecciones presidenciales de agosto de 1994:

Entre el escepticismo y la esperanza. Un informe sobre las condiciones previas," Mexico City, August 19, 1994, 2.

20. Fidencio Gonzáles, telephone interview with author, August 22, 1994.

21. M. Tangeman, "Elections Highlight Split in Catholic Church," *Mexico Insight* (Mexico City) 2, no. 9 (October 9, 1994): 8–9.

22. Ulises Hernández and Hector A. González, "Muñoz Rocha y narcos, solo brazos ejecutores de políticos de altas esferas," *El Financiero* (Mexico City), October 8, 1994, 9.

23. M. Tangeman, "Mexican Hierarchy, Orders at Odds," CNS cable in *National Catholic Reporter,* April 27, 1990.

24. Adolfo Suárez Rivera, interview with author, Cuernavaca, Mexico, October 27, 1994.

25. Carlos Quintero Arce, interview with author, Cuernavaca, Mexico, October 27, 1994.

26. Carlos Salinas de Gortari, quoted in Sallie Hughes, "Mexican Stand-Off," *El Financiero International Edition* (Mexico City), November 7–13, 1994, 14.

27. Juan Antonio Zuñiga M., "79.1% del déficit en cuenta corriente del 94 se cubrió con reservas," *La Jornada* (Mexico City), January 23, 1994, 52, 42.

28. Ernesto Zedillo, inaugural speech, "Suceso presidencial," *Reforma* (Mexico City), December 2, 1994, 7-I.

29. Sallie Hughes, "Two Governors, Two Armies," *El Financiero International Edition* (Mexico City), December 12–18, 1994, 1.

30. Joel Padrón, telephone interview with author, December 19, 1994.

31. Marco A. Cobos, "Crece deuda externa de Mexico en 75%," *Reforma* (Mexico City), January 7, 1995, 12-A.

32. Rodolfo Reyes, "Diálogo y claridad, pide la Iglesia de Tabasco al PRD y PRI," *El Financiero* (Mexico City), January 17, 1995, 49.

33. Francisco Goitia, telephone interview with author, January 19, 1995.

34. Lorenzo Meyer, telephone interview with author, January 19, 1995.

35. "Programa de Trabajo, Casos: Juan Jesús Posadas Ocampo, Luis Donaldo Colosio Murrieta, José Francisco Ruiz Massieu," Mexican Attorney General's Office, press bulletin, January 4, 1995, 5.

36. Hector A. González, "'Avances significativos' en las investigaciones: Chapa Benzanilla," *El Financiero* (Mexico City) January 12, 1995, 36; Irma Salas, "Analizan homicidio Chapa y Sandoval," *Reforma* (Mexico City), January 17, 1995, 2-A.

37. Ismael Romero, "Enfrentar la violencia que existe en el país como un problema estructural, piden curas a Moctezuma," *La Jornada* (Mexico City), January 6, 1995, 11.

38. Tomás de la Rosa, "Baja 69 por ciento salario mínimo real," *Reforma* (Mexico City), January 16, 1995, A-1.

39. Lourdes Edith Rudiño, "Manejo inadecuado del concepto Procampo realizaron las autoridades en el acuerdo," *El Financiero* (Mexico City), January 6, 1995, 25.

40. "En el trato con Estados Unidos de América la soberanía de México no es un tema sujeto a discusión," press bulletin, Office of the Mexican Presidency, January 21, 1995.

41. Julio Fentanes and Hugo Calderón, "Piden no generalizar problemas electorales," *Reforma* (Mexico City) January 24, 1995, 4-A.

Index

131